# Sugar Skulls 2
## Zany Robots, Aliens, Animals & More!

SHANNON DUFFY

This book is dedicated to my sons, Dakota and Dylan

## PROJECT IDEAS

The designs in this book can be used for more than just coloring fun. Use them as ideas for shrink art designs, glass etching inspiration or even your own meringue powder sugar skull design creations.

The designs may be used for non-commercial, inspirational use only.

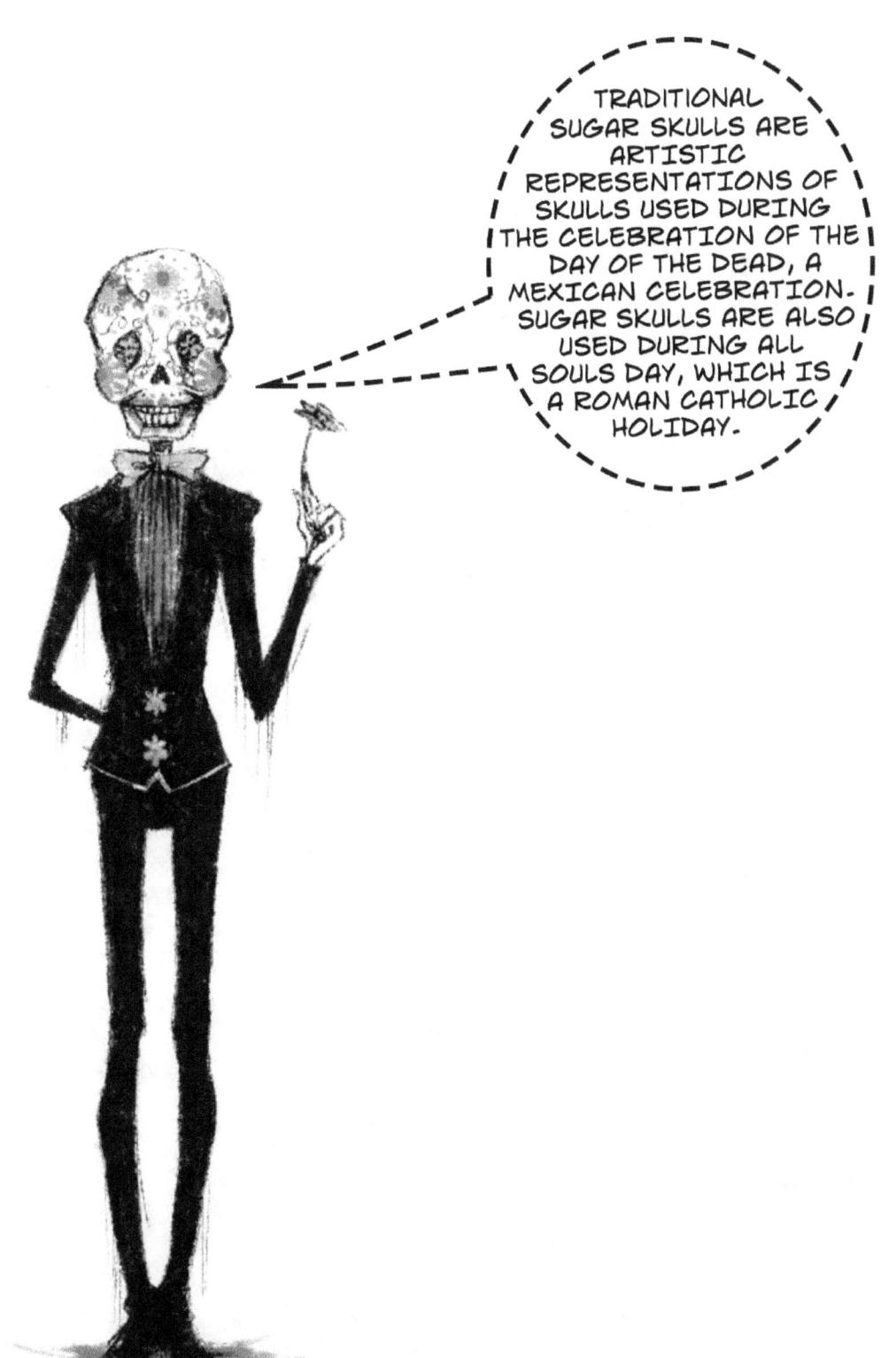

# MAKE YOUR OWN 3 INGREDIENT SUGAR SKULL:

**1** IN A MEDIUM SIZED MIXING BOWL, WHISK THE GRANULATED SUGAR AND MERINGUE POWDER TOGETHER.

INGREDIENTS:
1 1/2 TEASPOONS WATER
2 TEASPOONS MERINGUE POWDER
1 CUP GRANULATED SUGAR

**3** ONCE COMBINED AND THE CONSISTENCY OF A FIRM PASTE, BEGIN FORMING THE MIXTURE INTO A BALL SHAPE.

**2** NEXT, ADD THE WATER AND BEGIN COMBINING THE INGREDIENTS TOGETHER EITHER WITH A WOODEN SPOON OR YOUR HANDS.

**4** WITH YOUR HANDS, BEGIN SHAPING THE BALL SHAPE INTO A SKULL FORM AND ADD TWO INDENTATIONS ON ONE SIDE TO FORM THE EYE SOCKETS.

**5** PLACE ON A JELLYROLL PAN, COOKIE SHEET OR EVEN A PIECE OF CARDBOARD AND ALLOW TO DRY OVERNIGHT.

**6** NOW THAT IT'S DRY, IT'S TIME TO DECORATE! YOU CAN USE BOTH EDIBLE AND NON-EDIBLE DECORATIONS TO FANCY UP YOUR NEW SUGAR SKULL CREATION. JUST REMEMBER TO REMOVE NON-EDIBLE PIECES BEFORE EATING!

**TIP #1** FOR BEST RESULTS, MAKE YOUR SUGAR SKULL ON A LOW HUMIDITY DAY. OTHERWISE, THE MIXTURE MAY NOT SET UP PROPERLY.

**TIP #2** YOU CAN ADD SMALL INCREMENTS OF WATER OR GRANULATED SUGAR TO ADJUST THE FIRMNESS OF THE MIXTURE IF IT DOESN'T SEEM TO BE FIRMING UP AS YOU BEGIN TO SHAPE IT.

**TIP #3** IN A HURRY? YOU CAN ALSO PUT YOUR NEWLY FORMED SUGAR SKULL IN THE OVEN AT 200 DEGREES FOR 10-20 MINUTES TO SPEED UP THE DRYING PROCESS BEFORE DECORATING!

**BE SAFE!** KIDS, BE SURE TO ONLY USE AN OVEN WITH ADULT SUPERVISION! SAFETY FIRST!

3

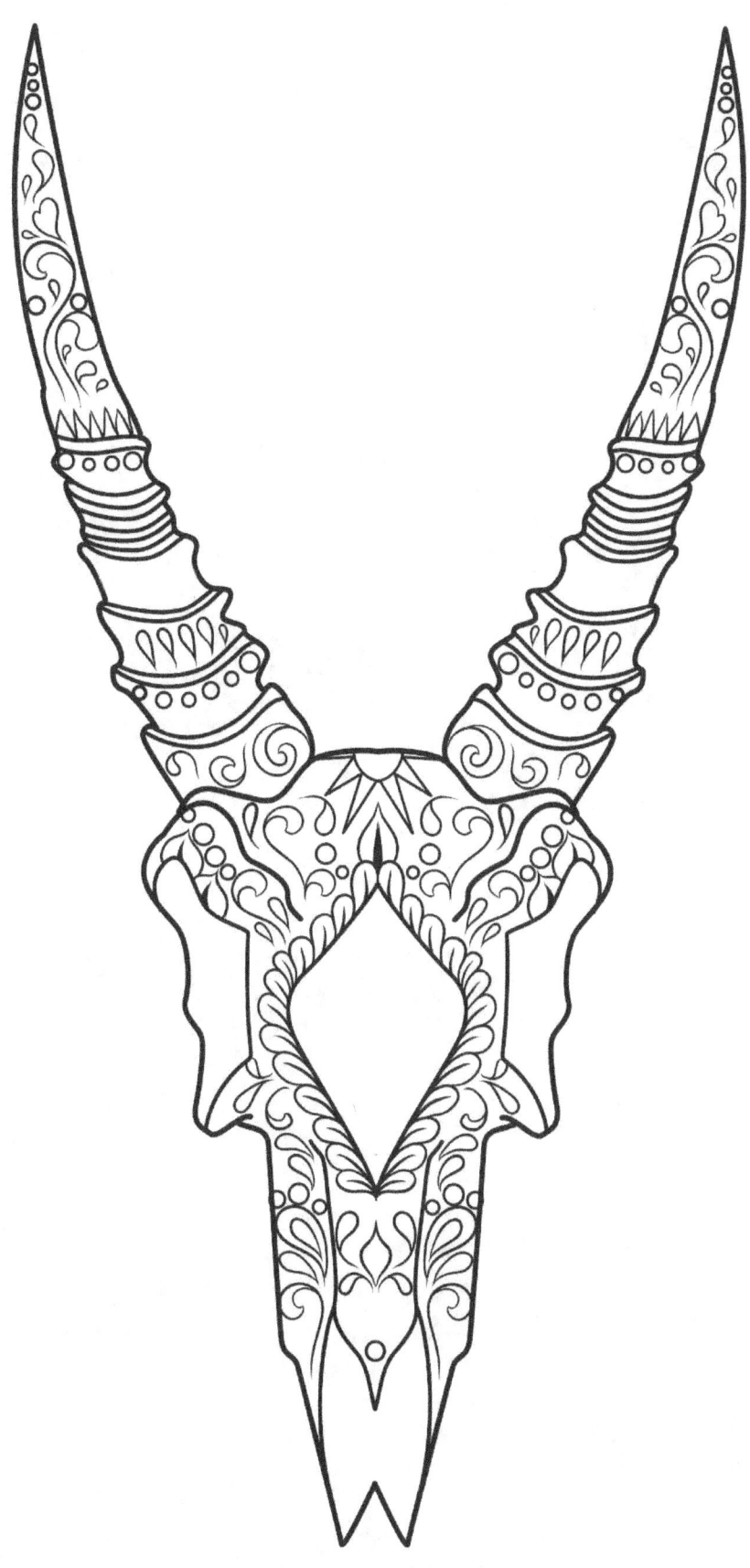

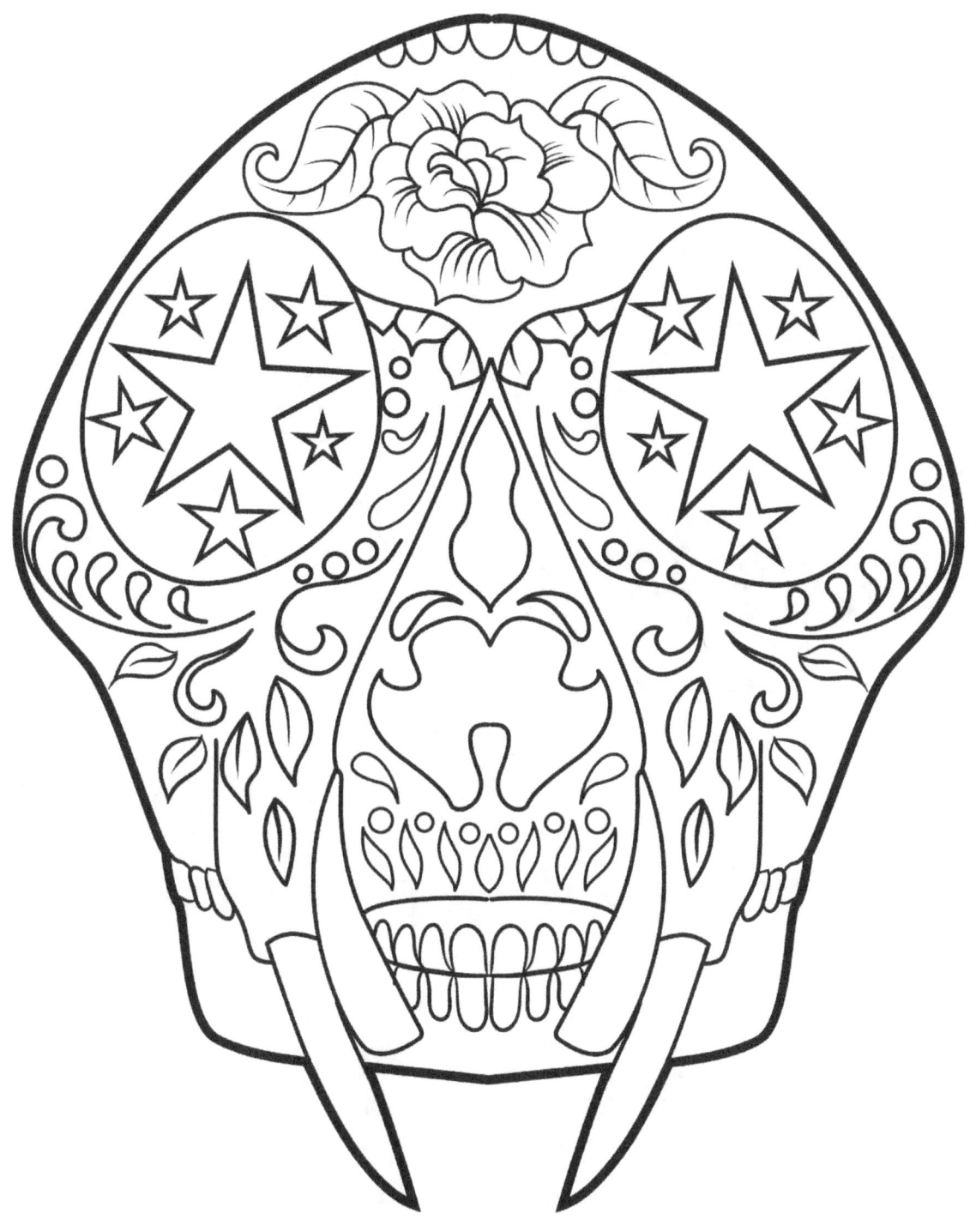

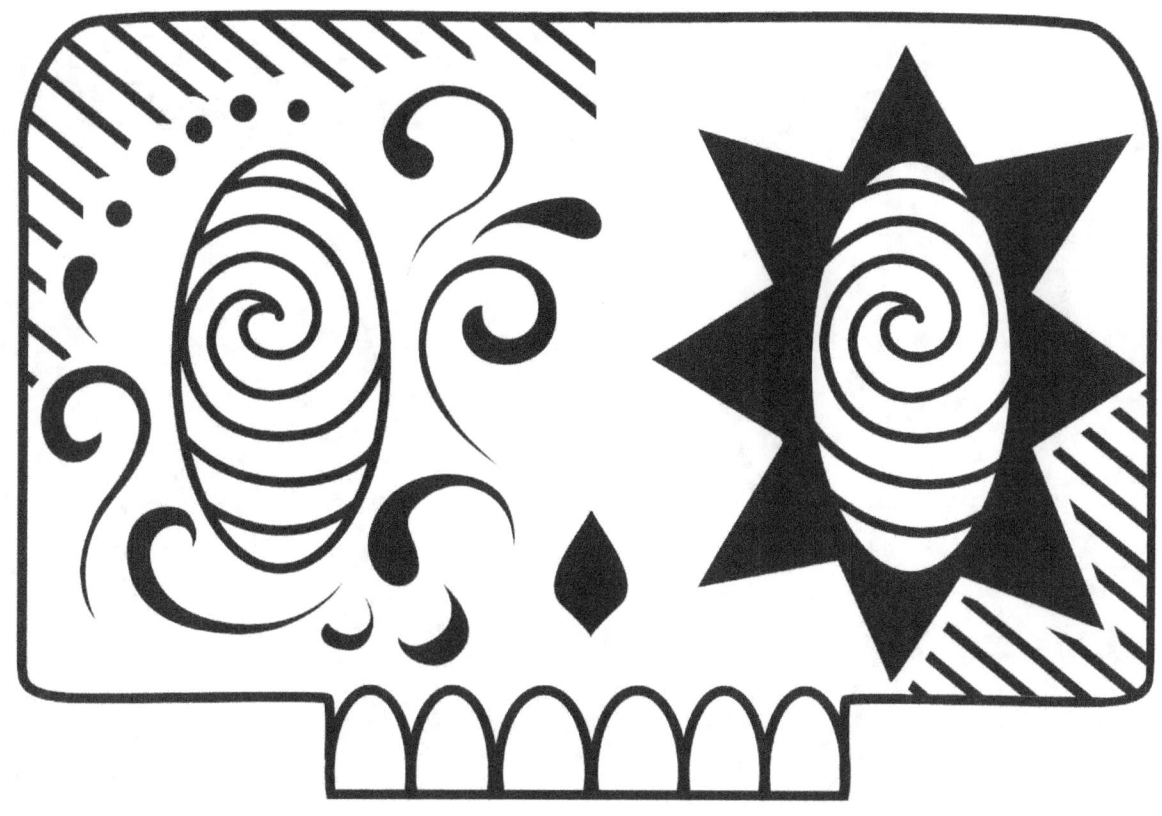

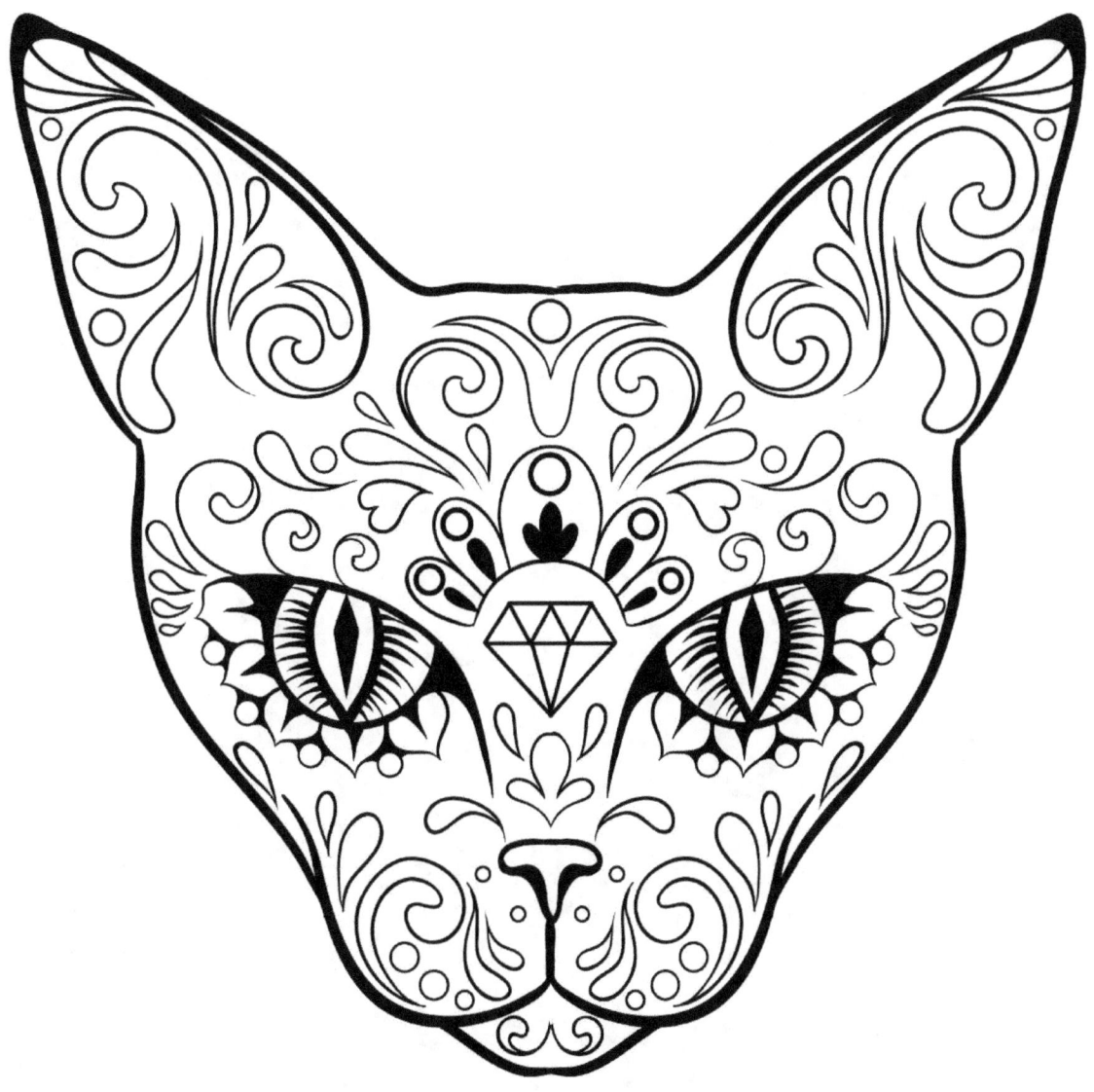

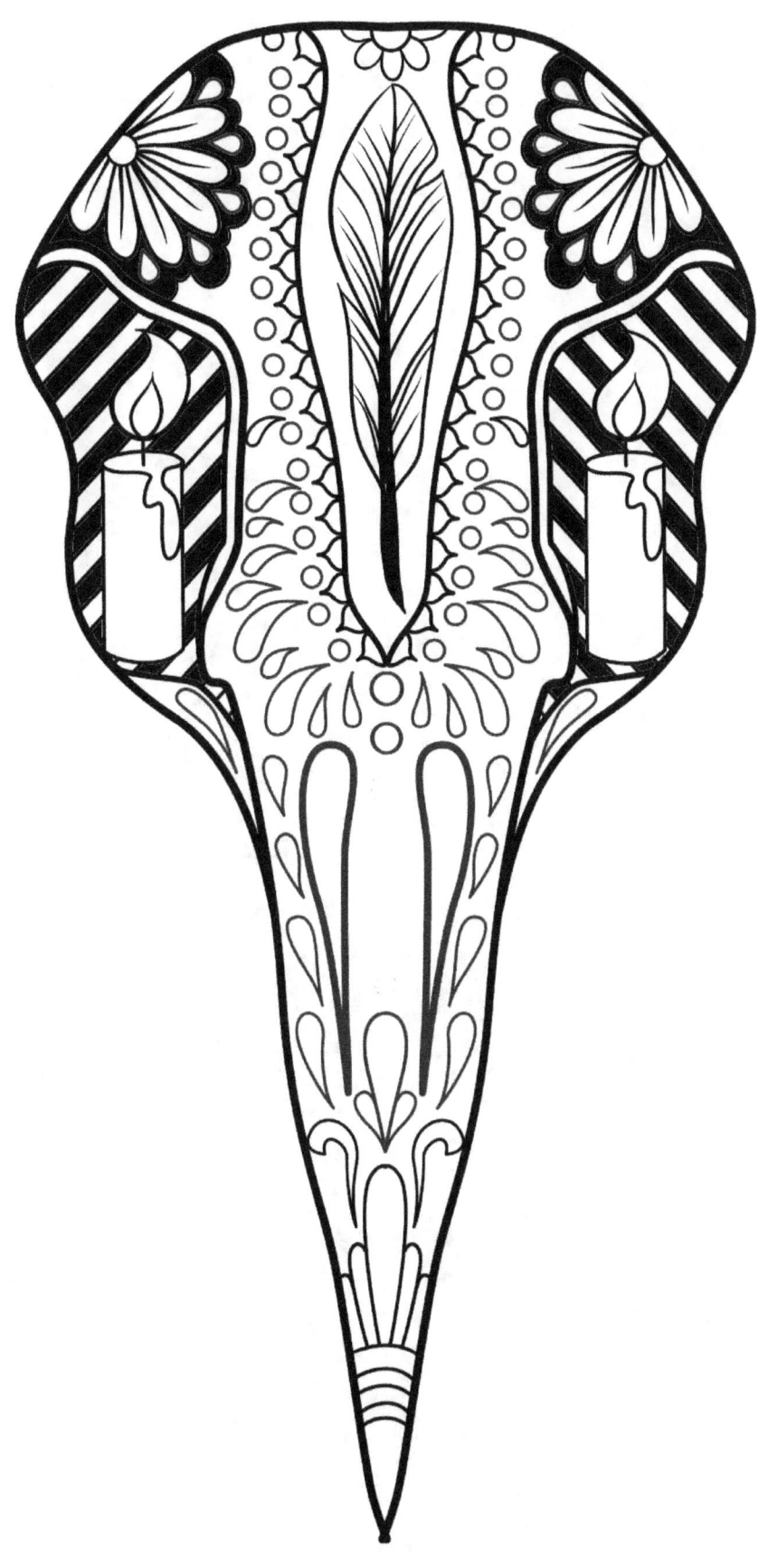

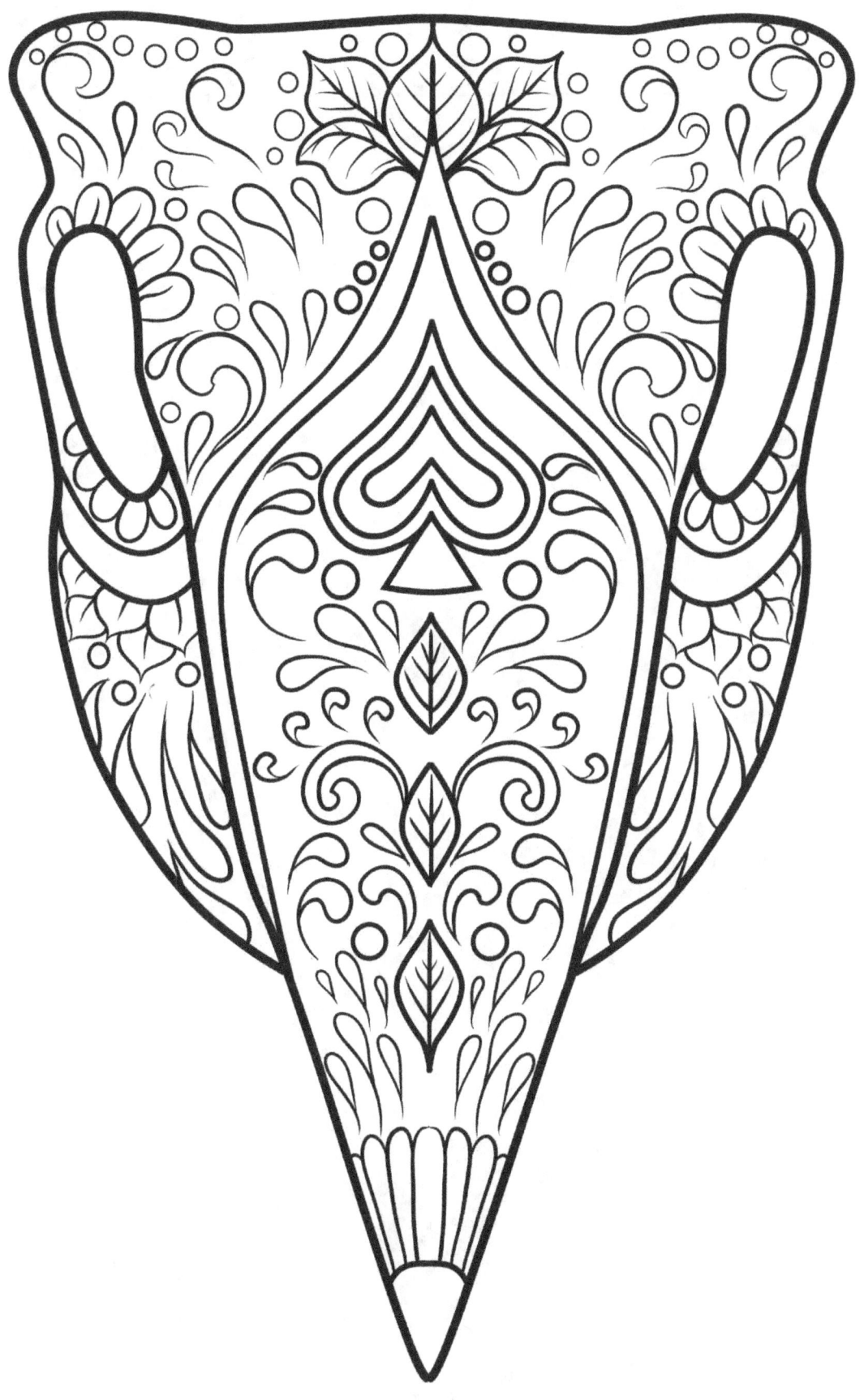

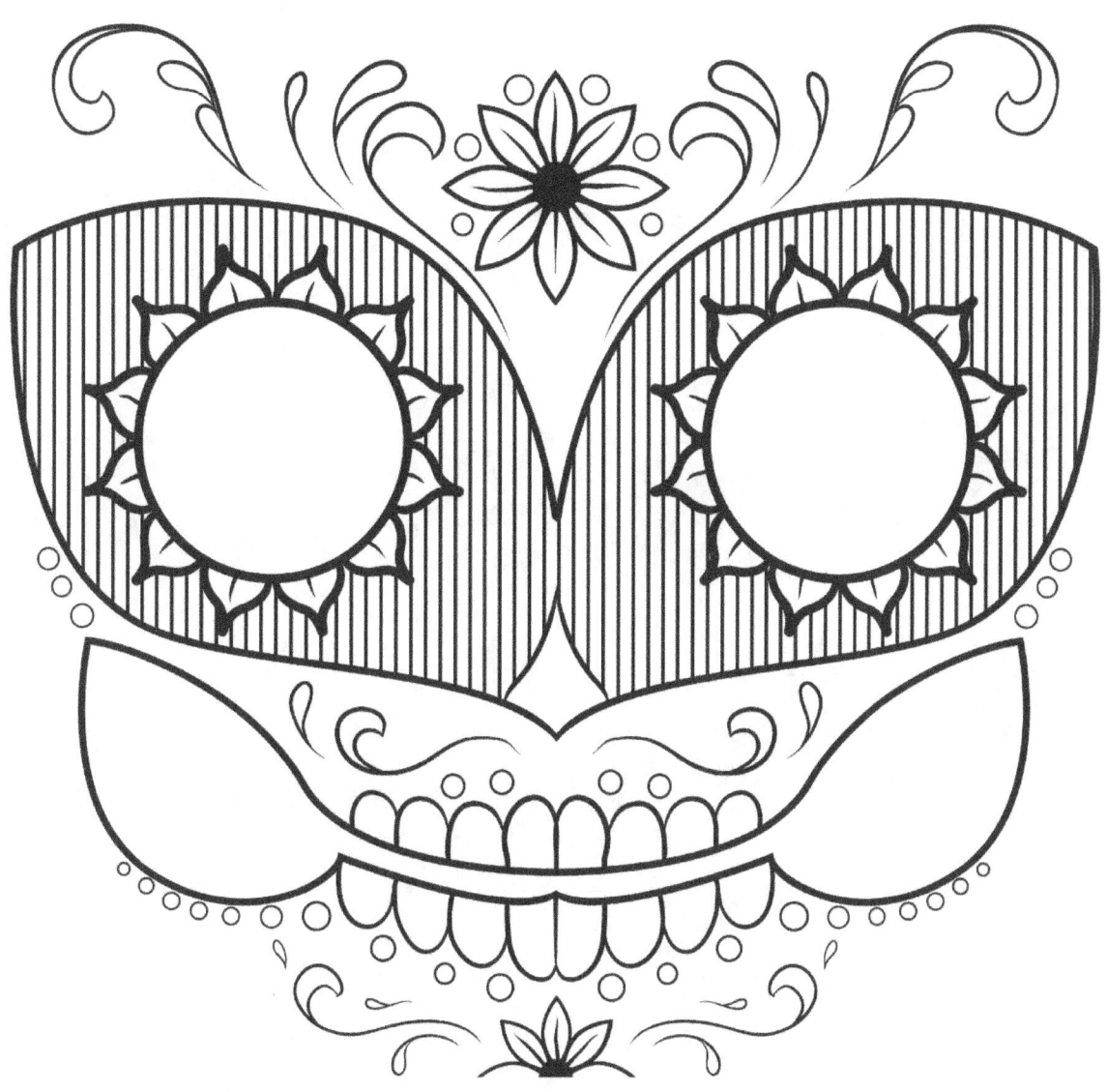

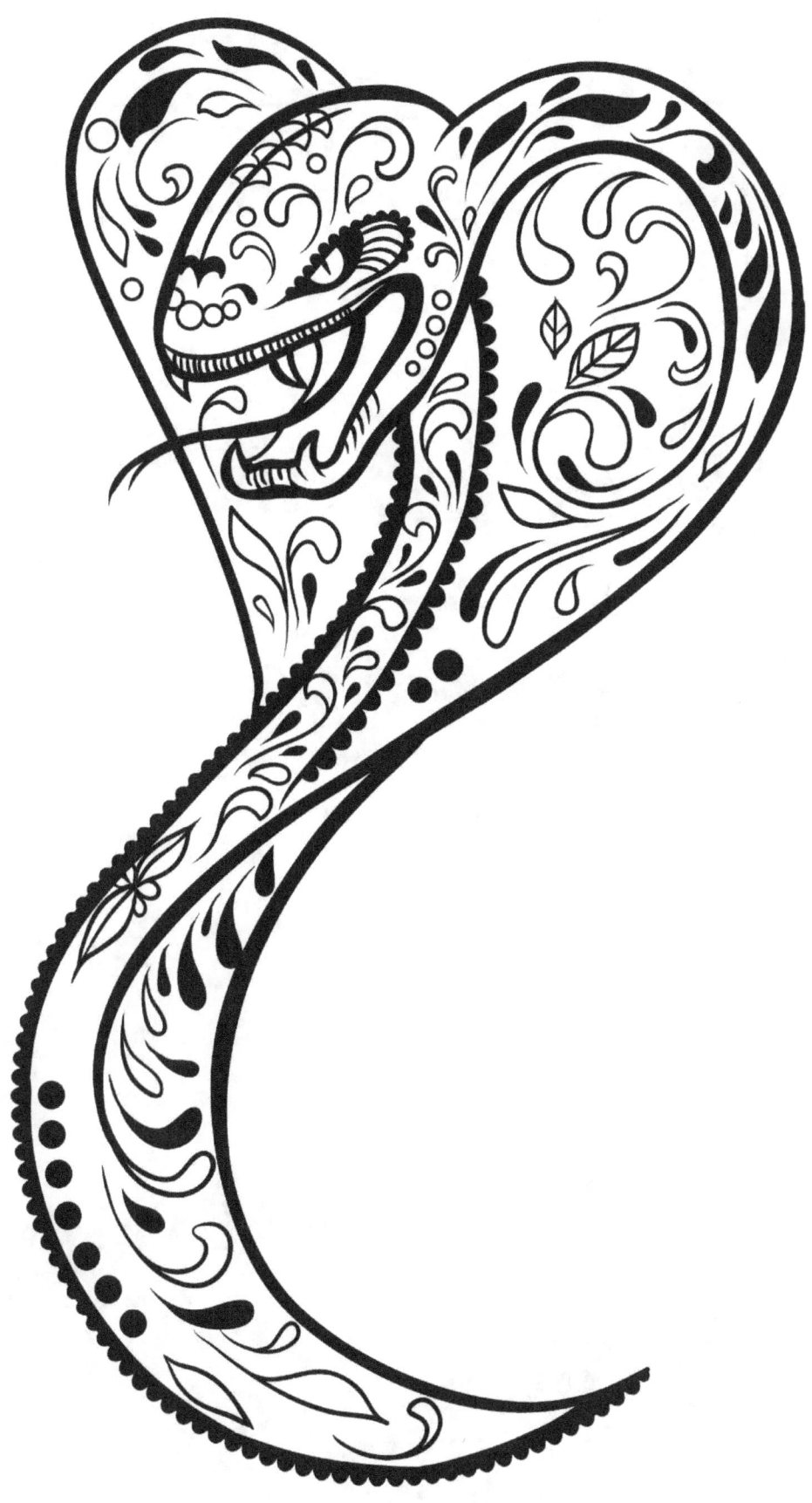

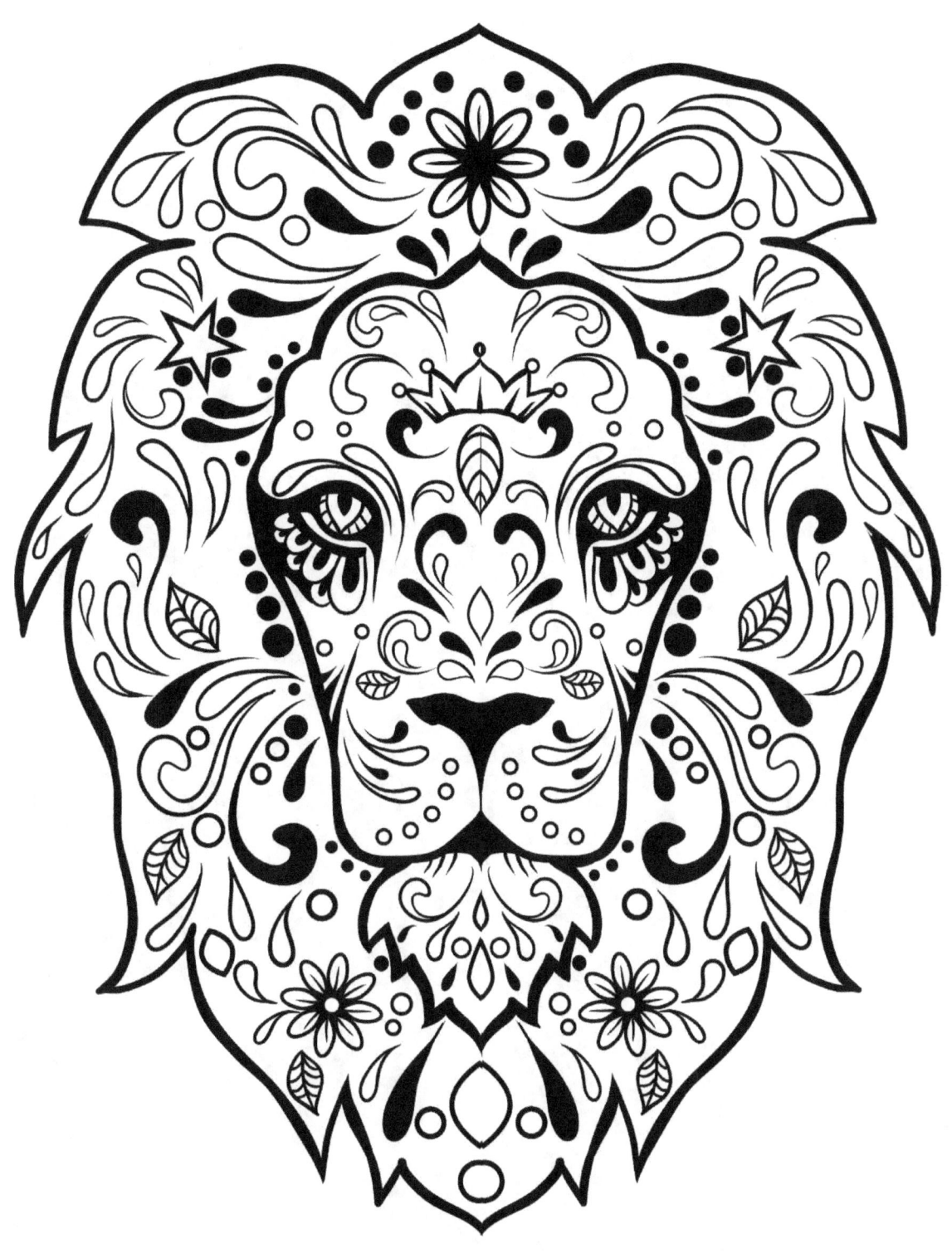

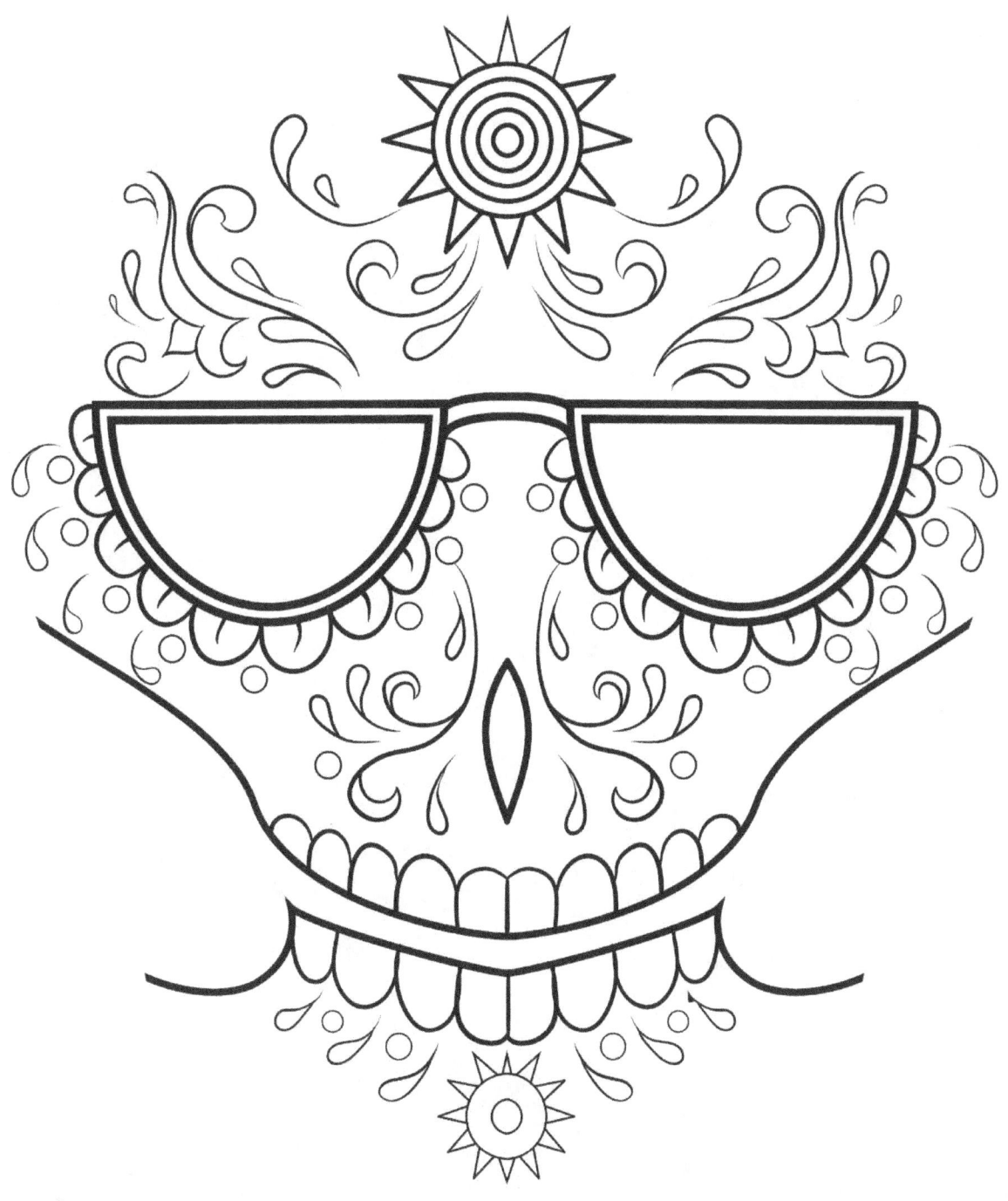

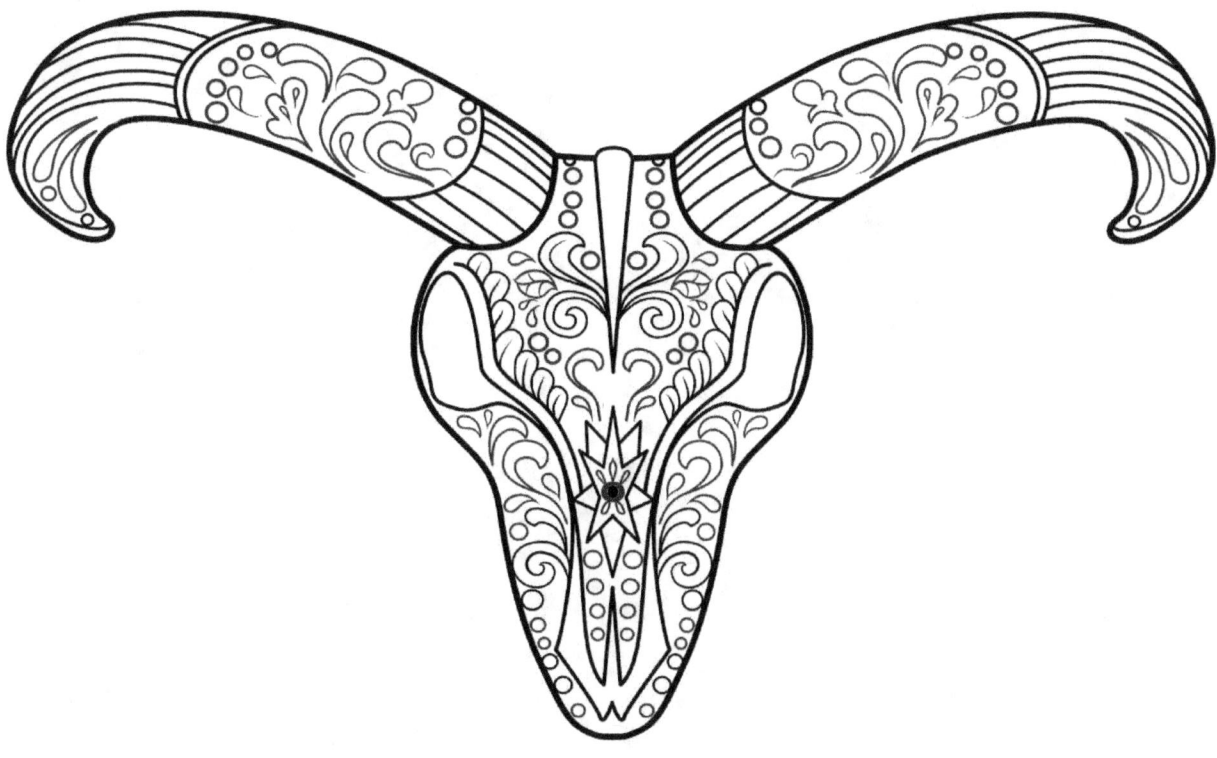

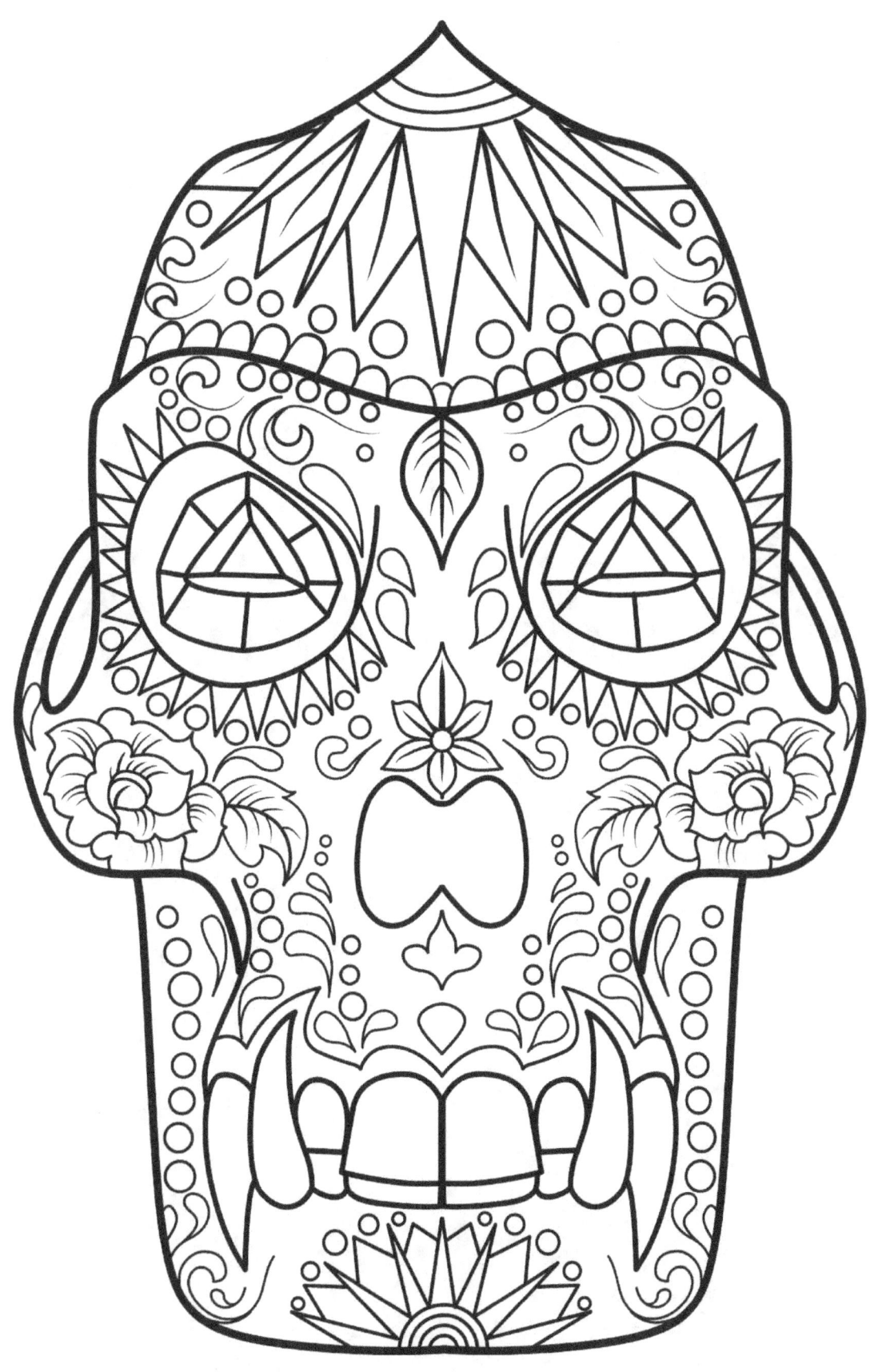

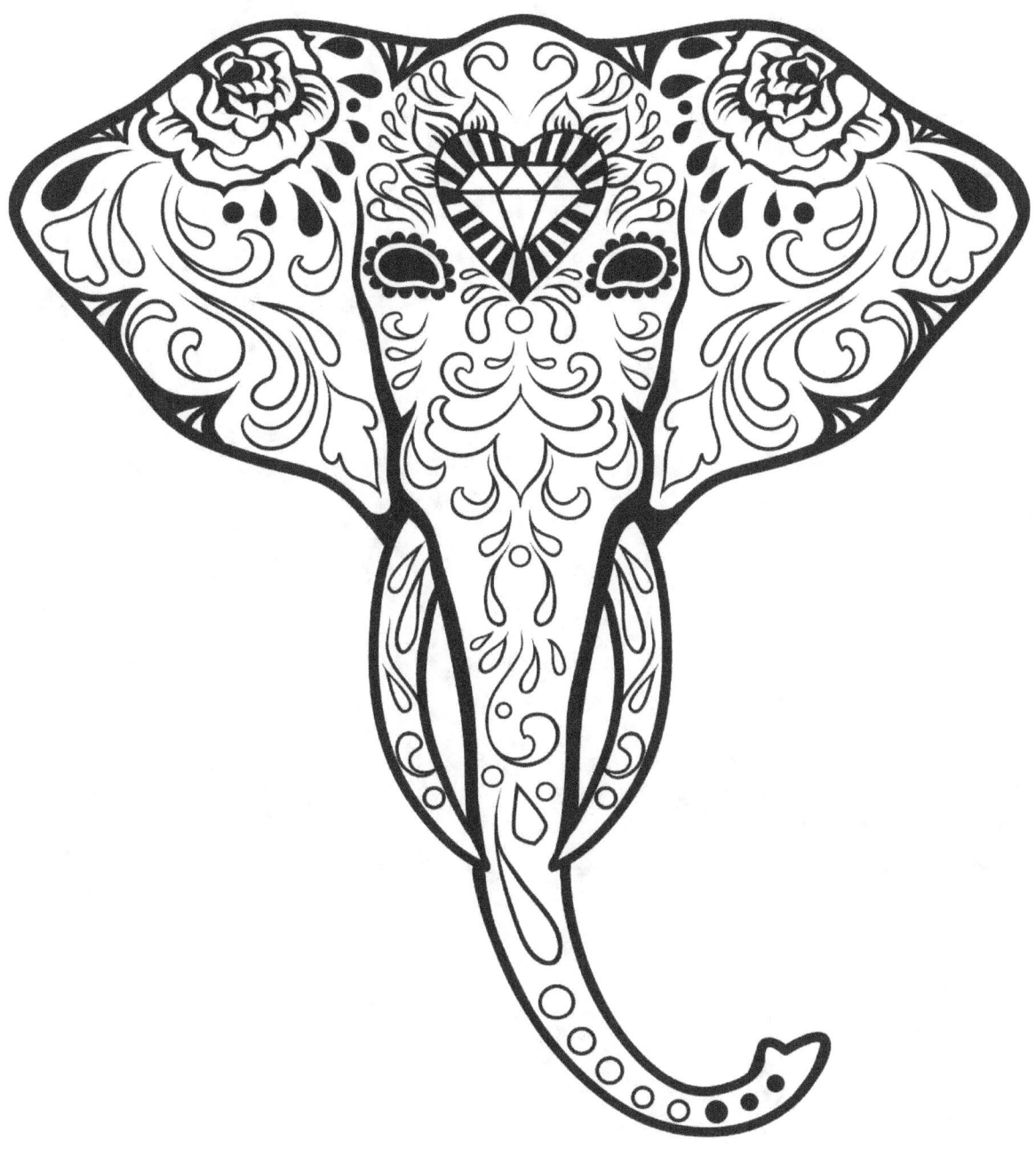

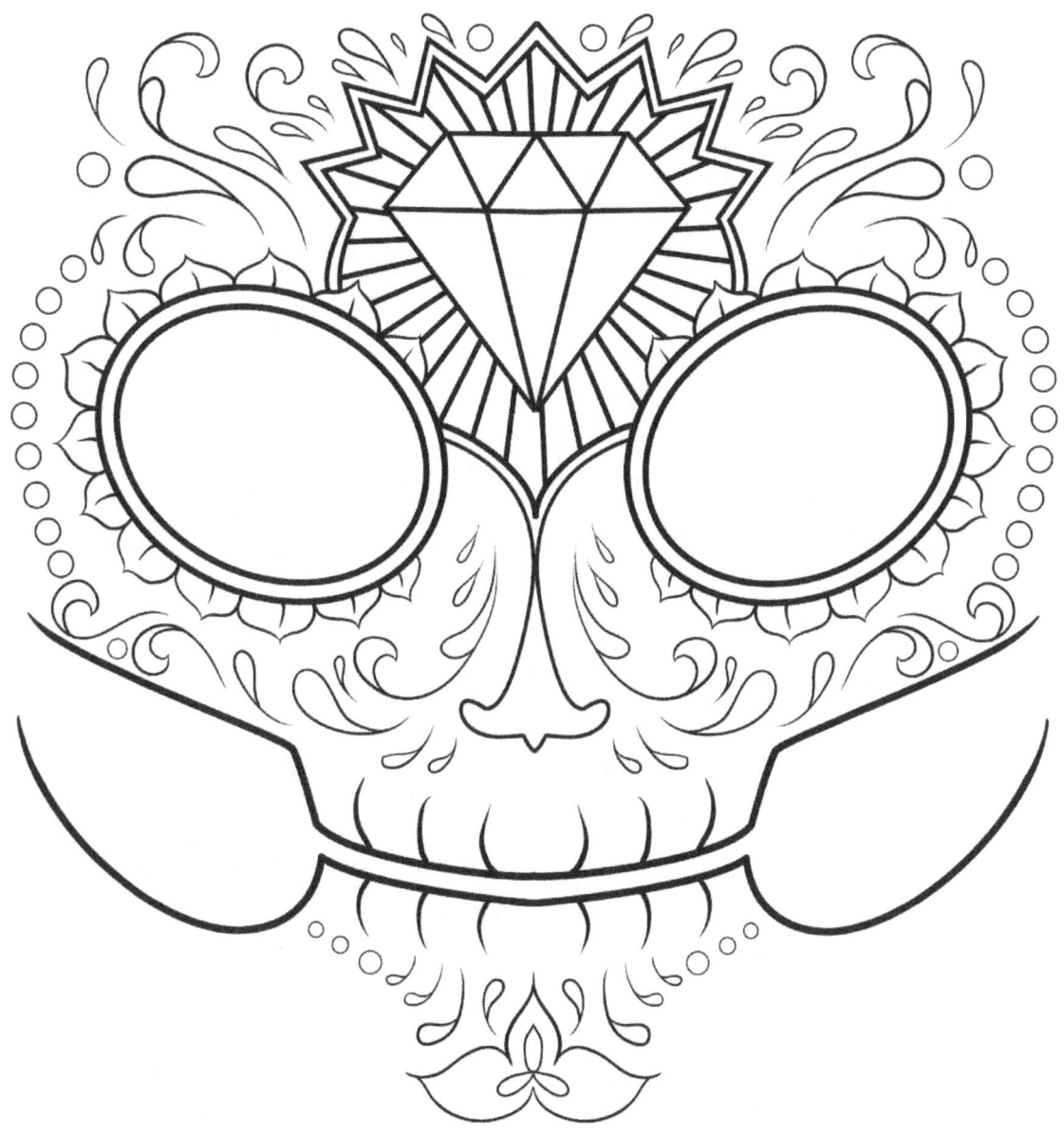

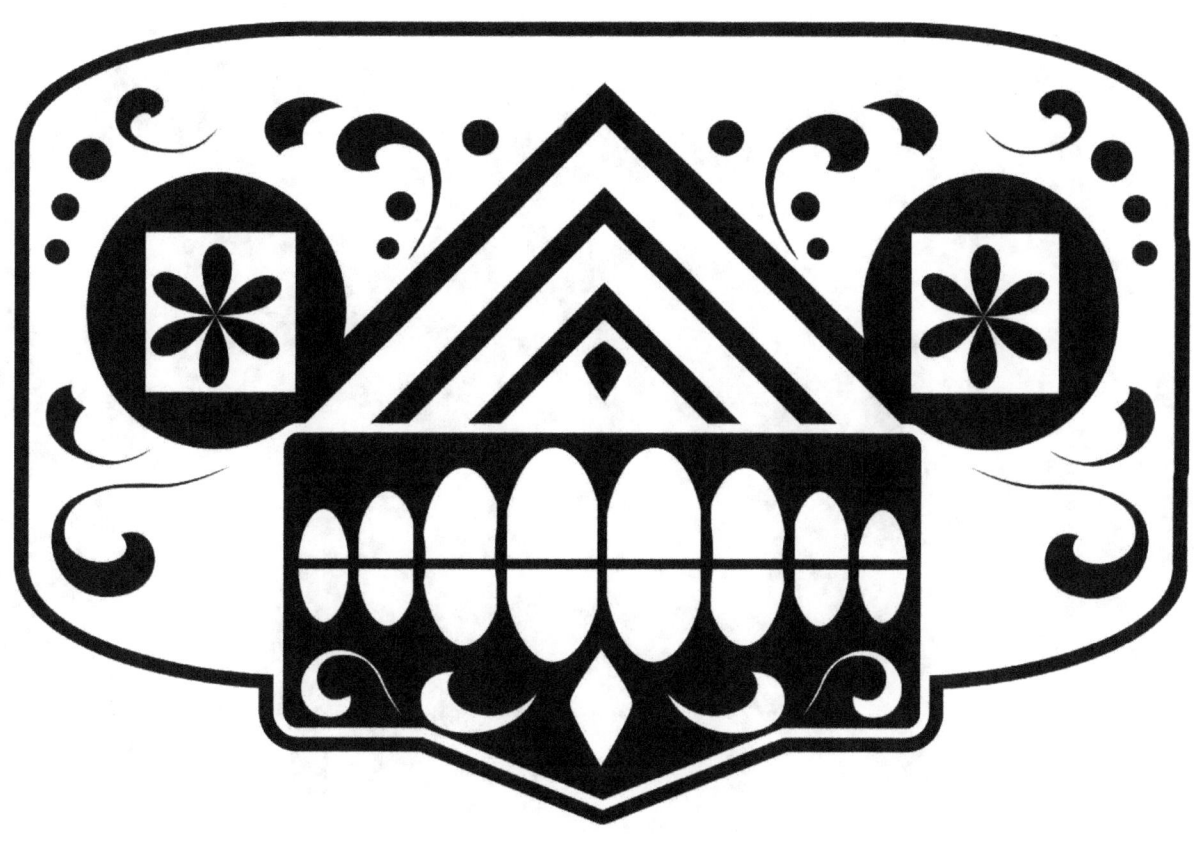

SUGAR SKULL 2 – ZANY ROBOTS, ALIENS, ANIMALS AND MORE!

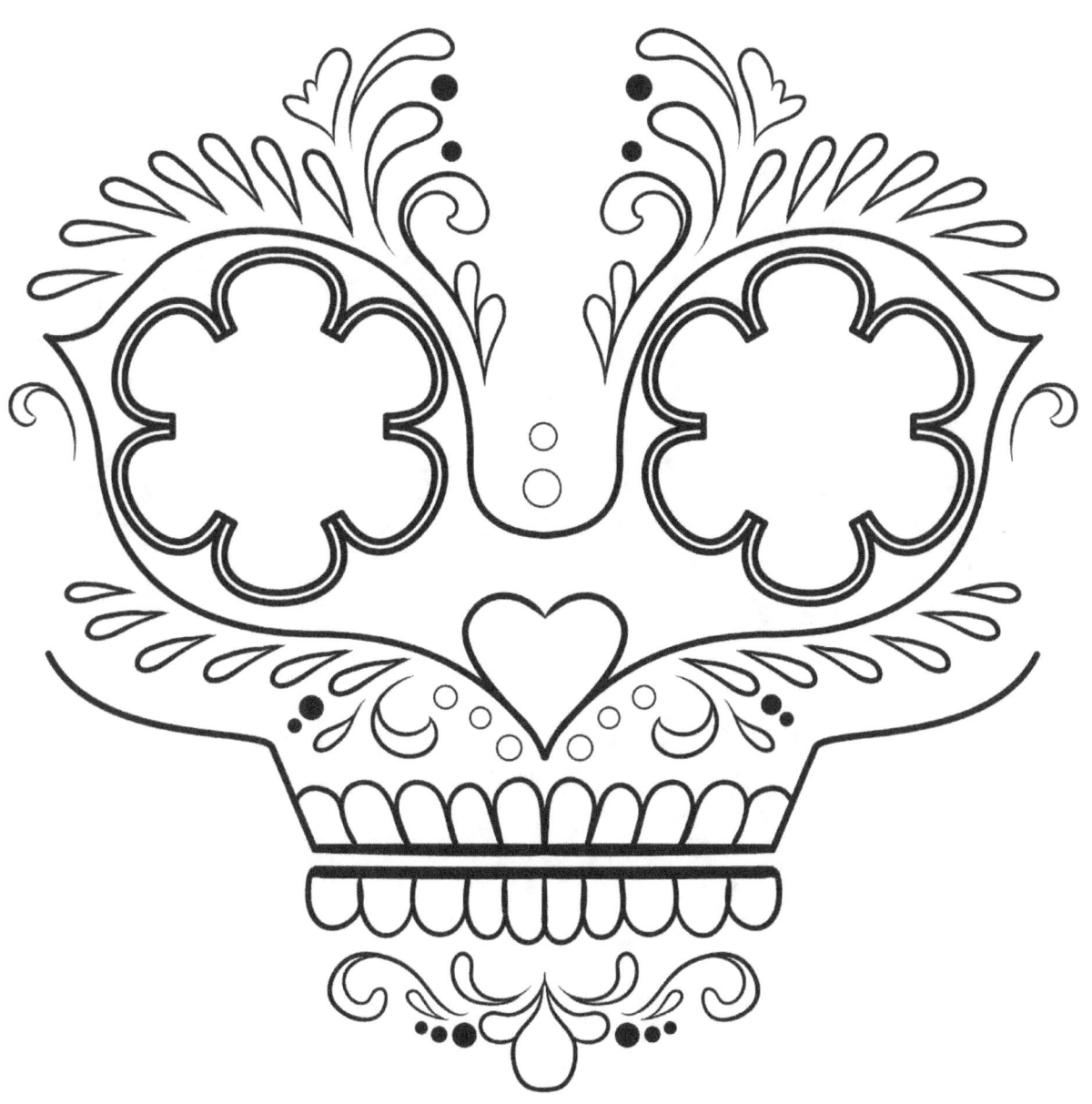

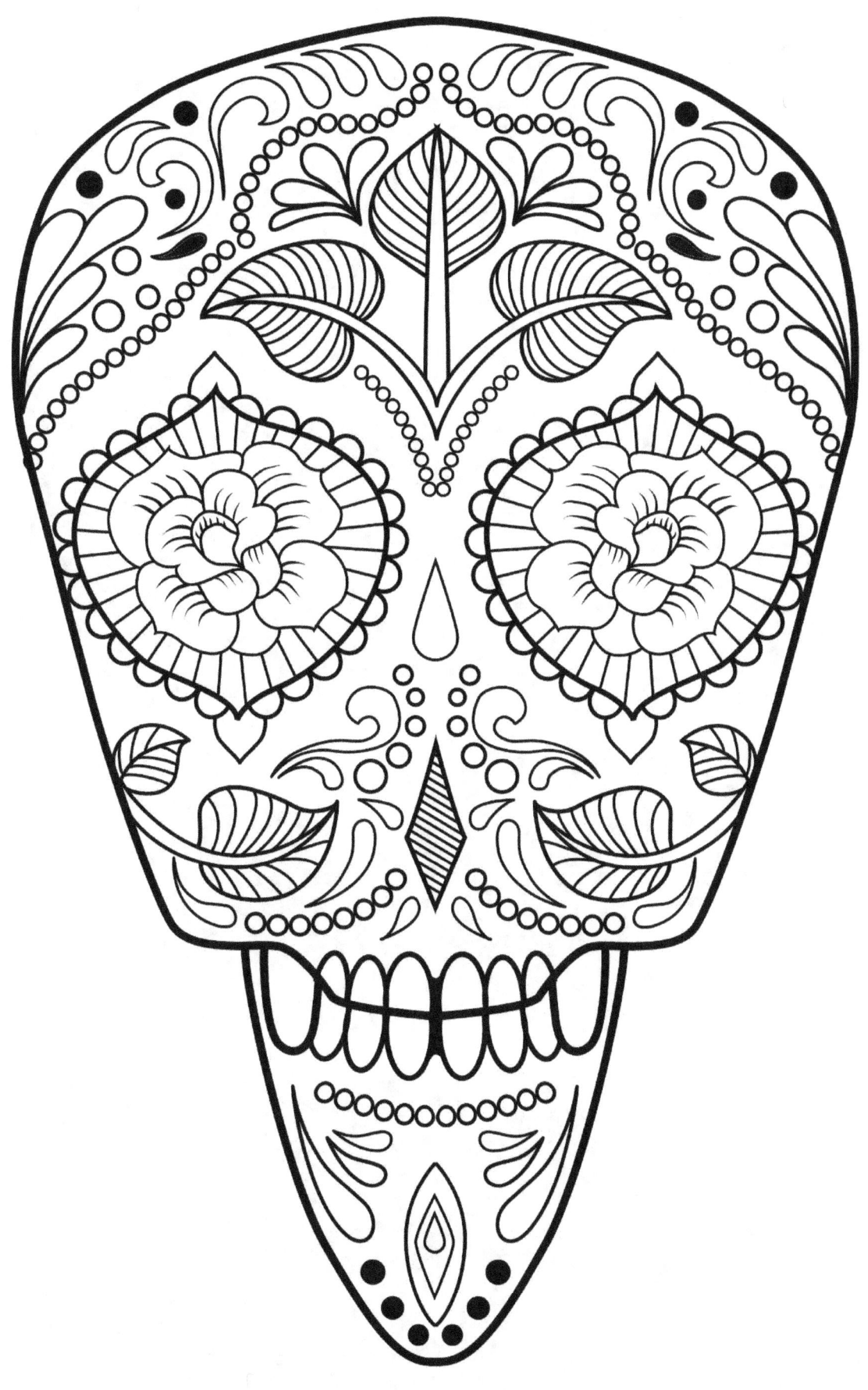

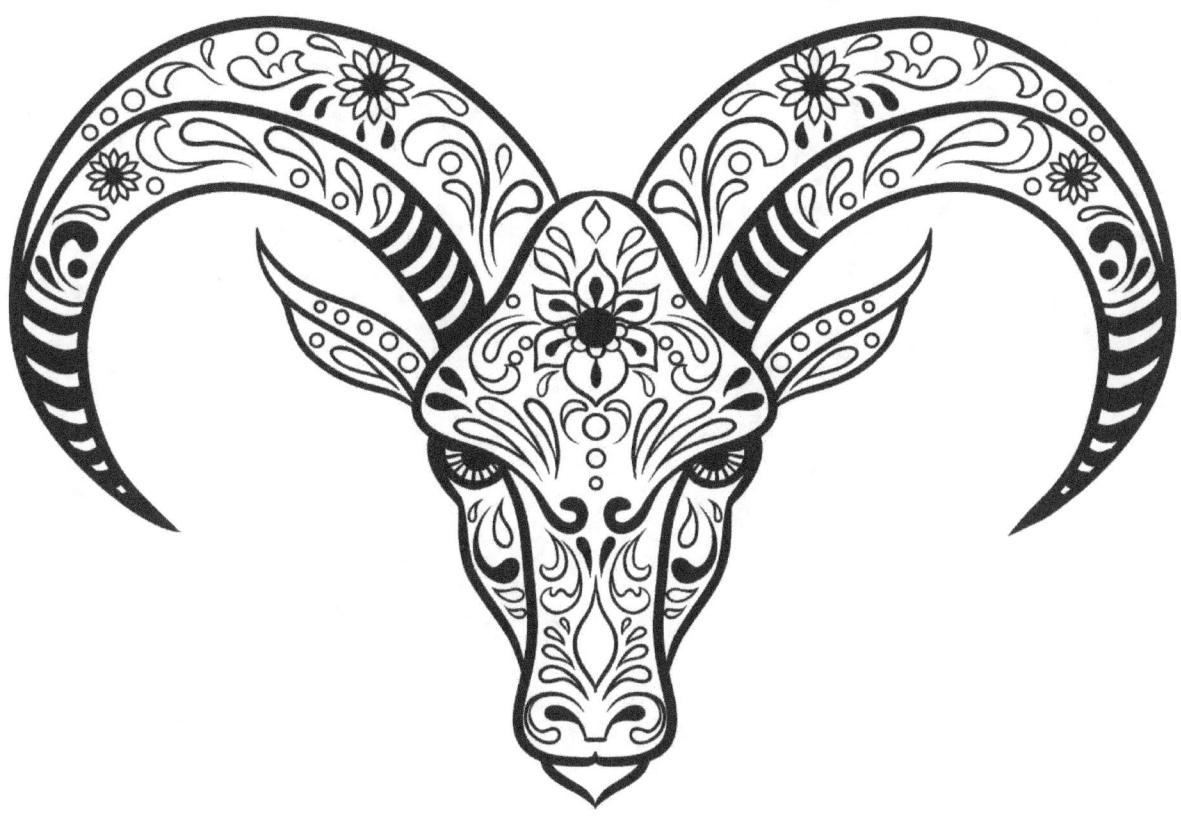

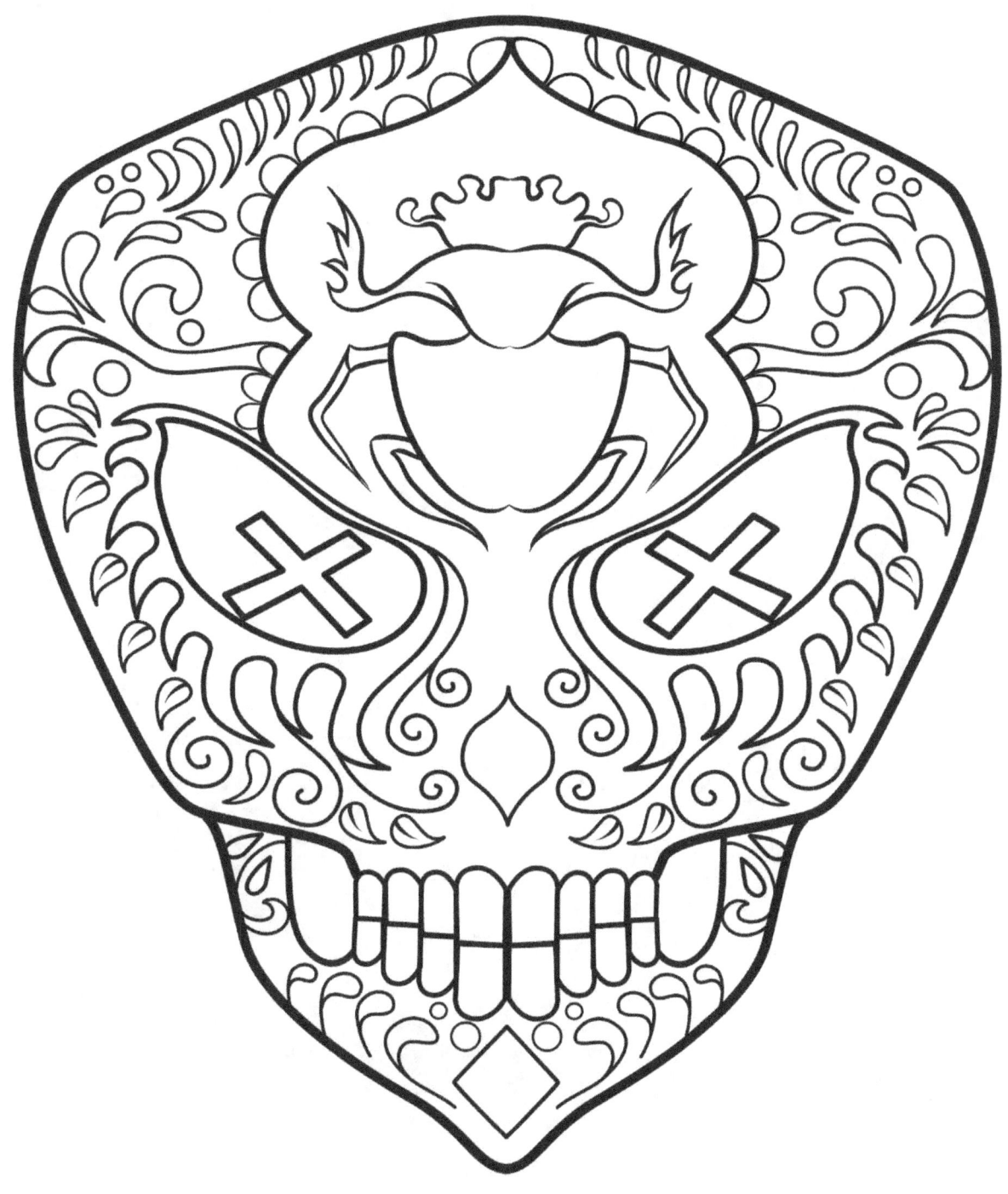

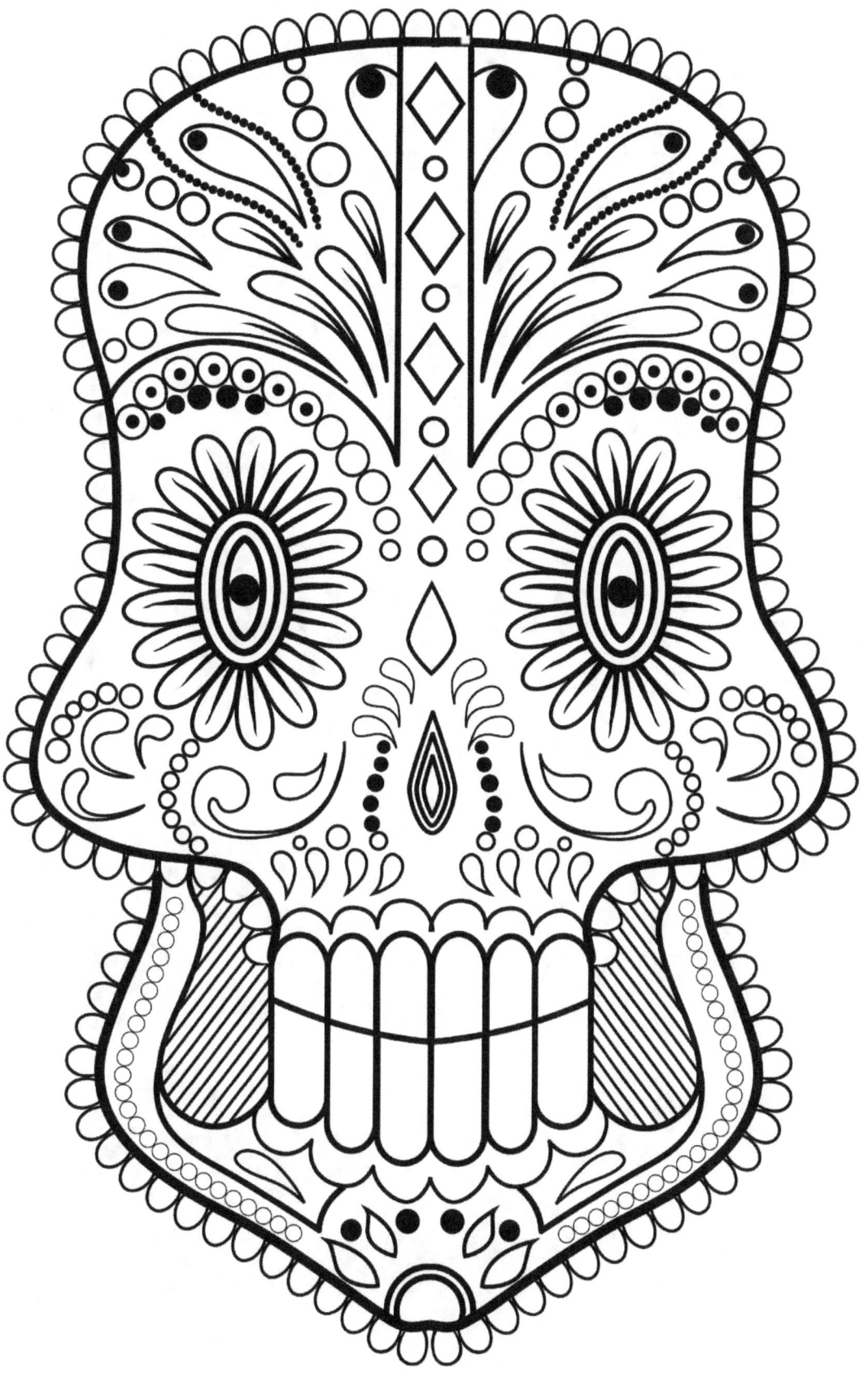

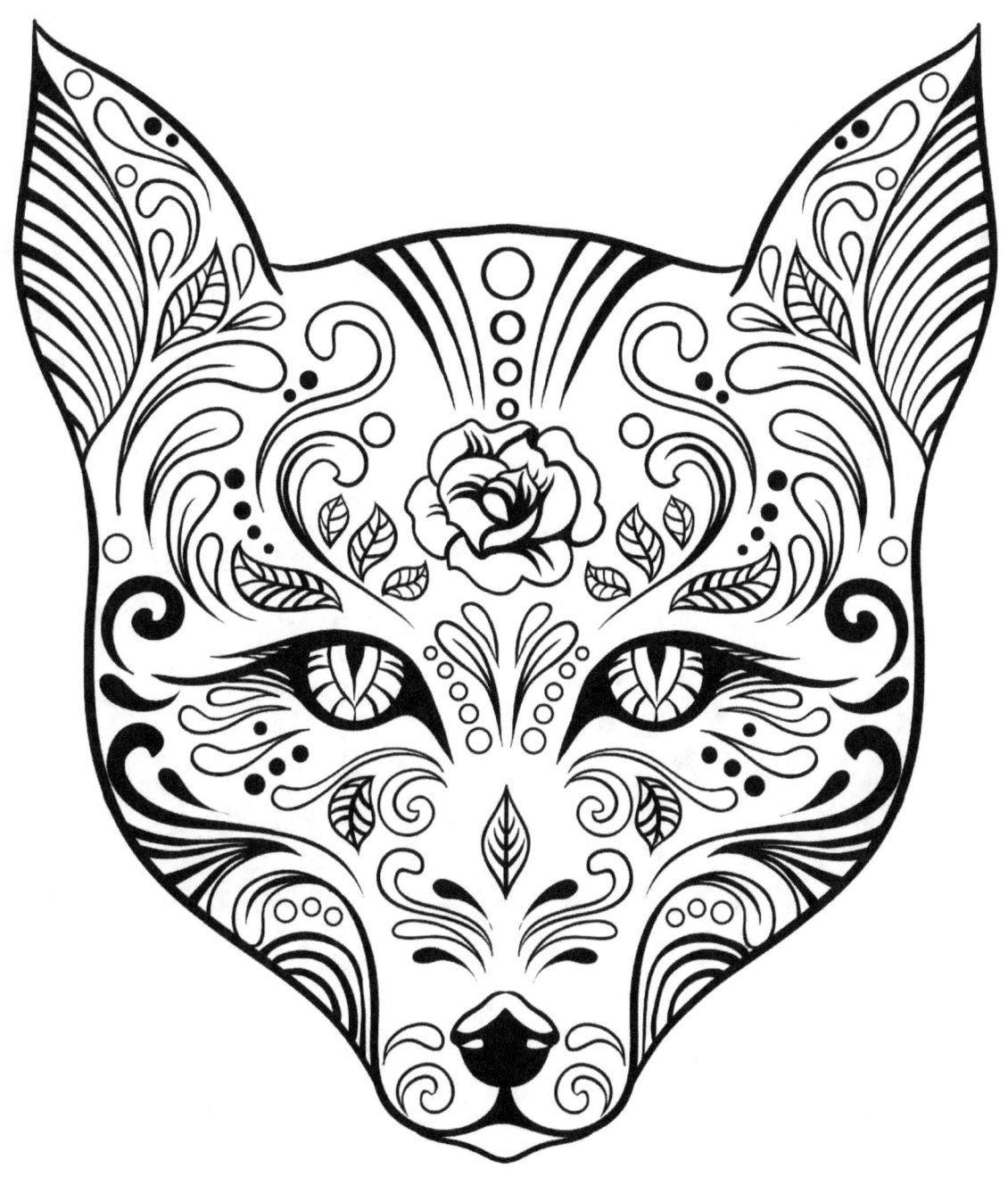

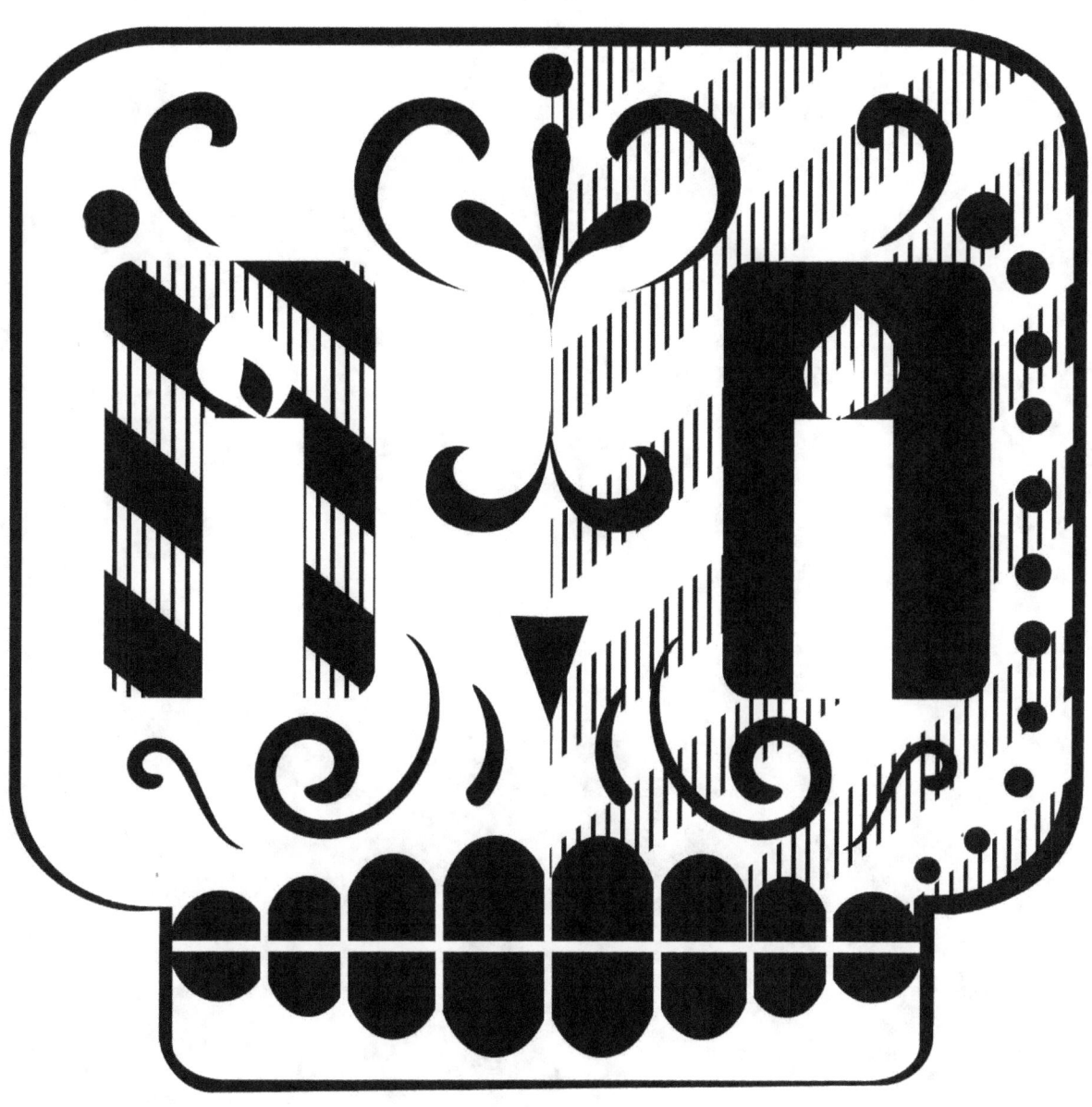

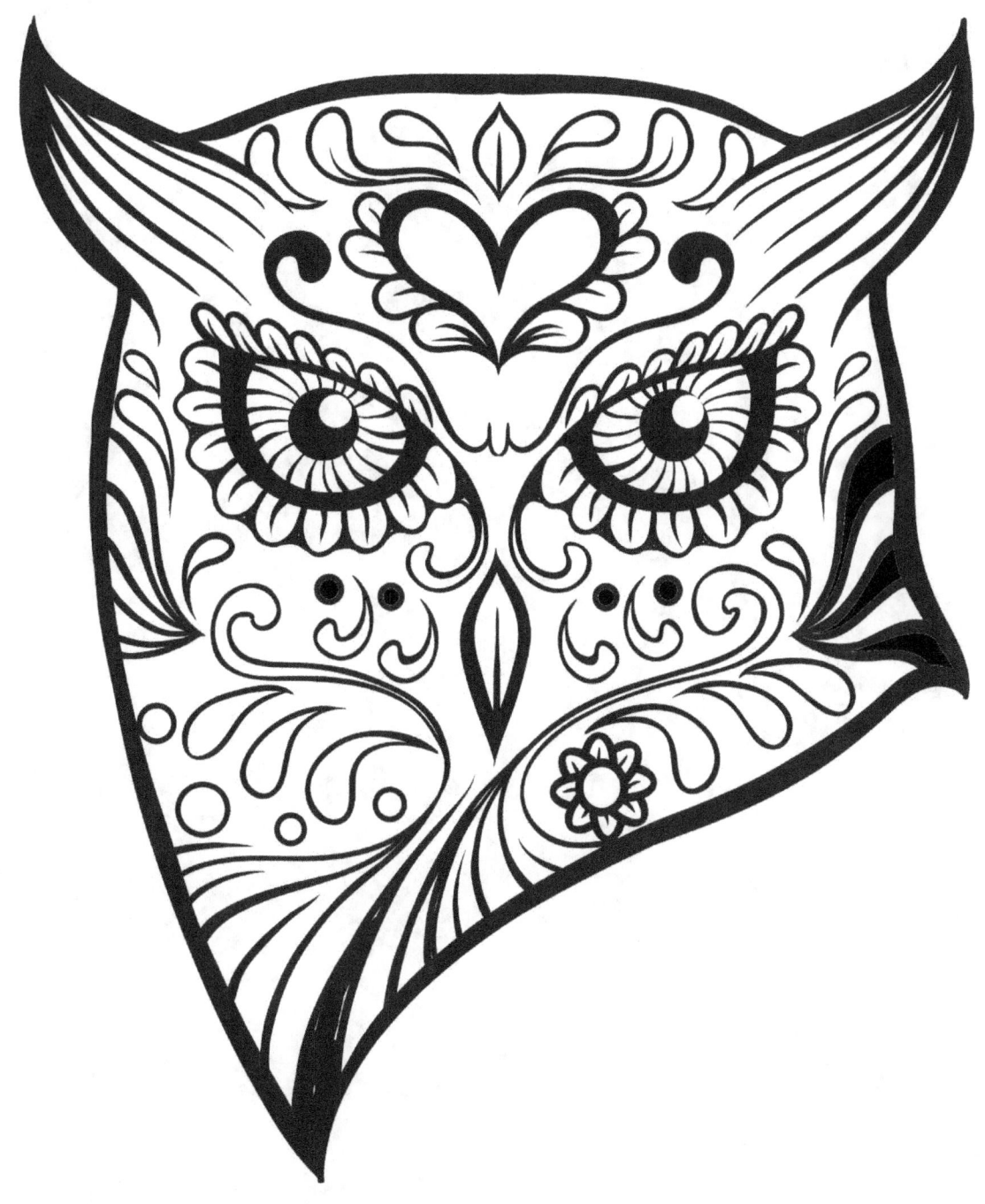

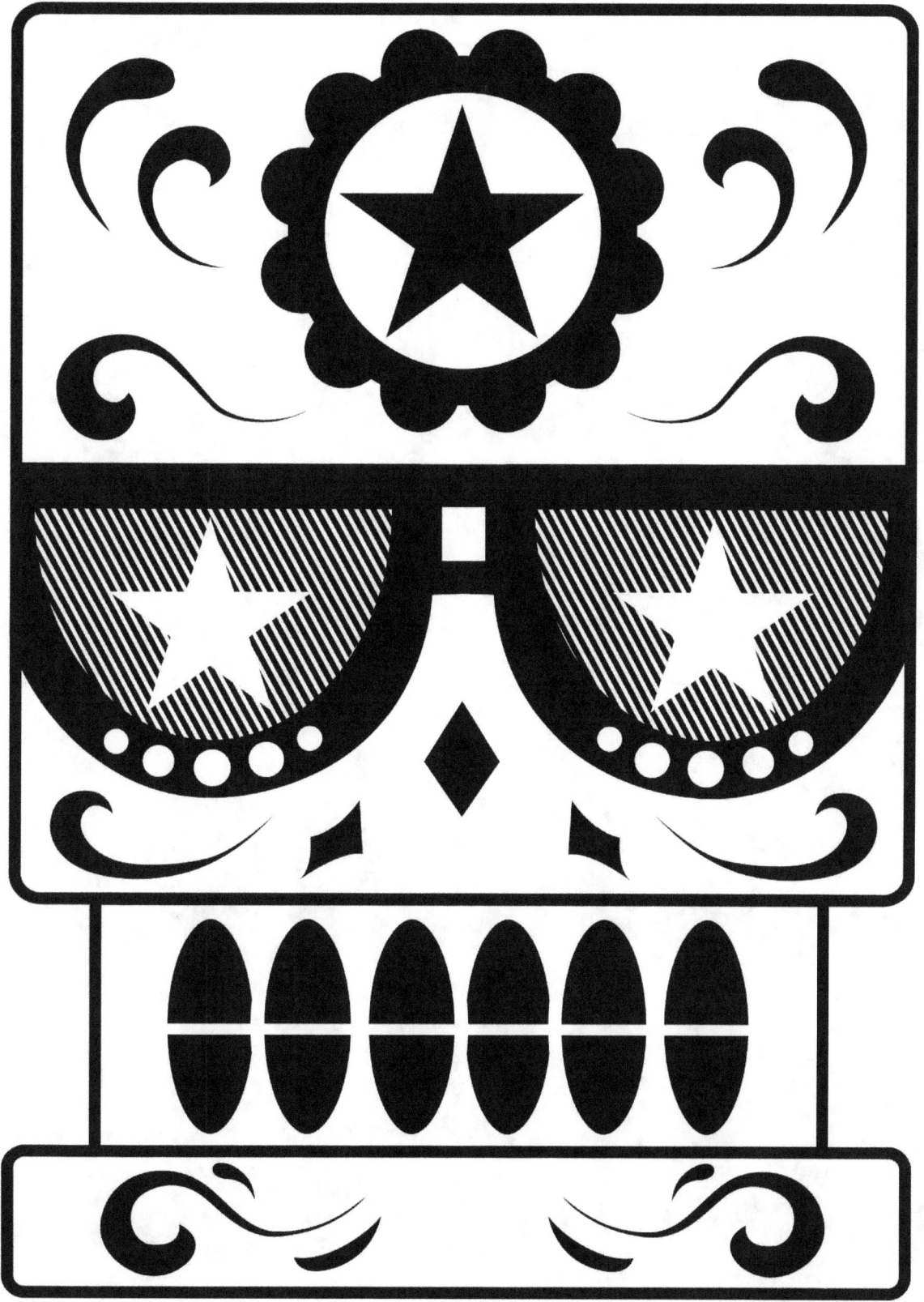

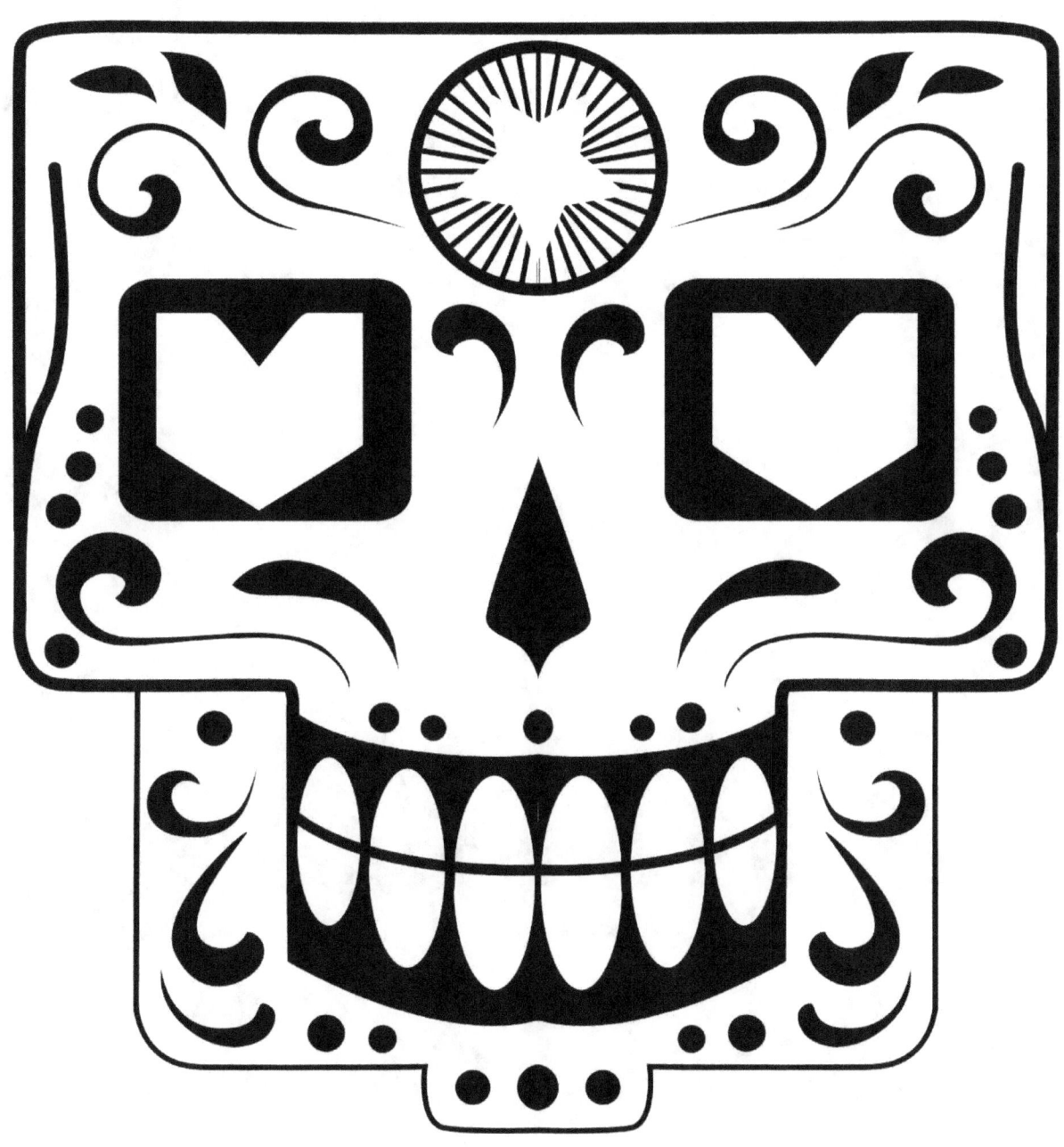

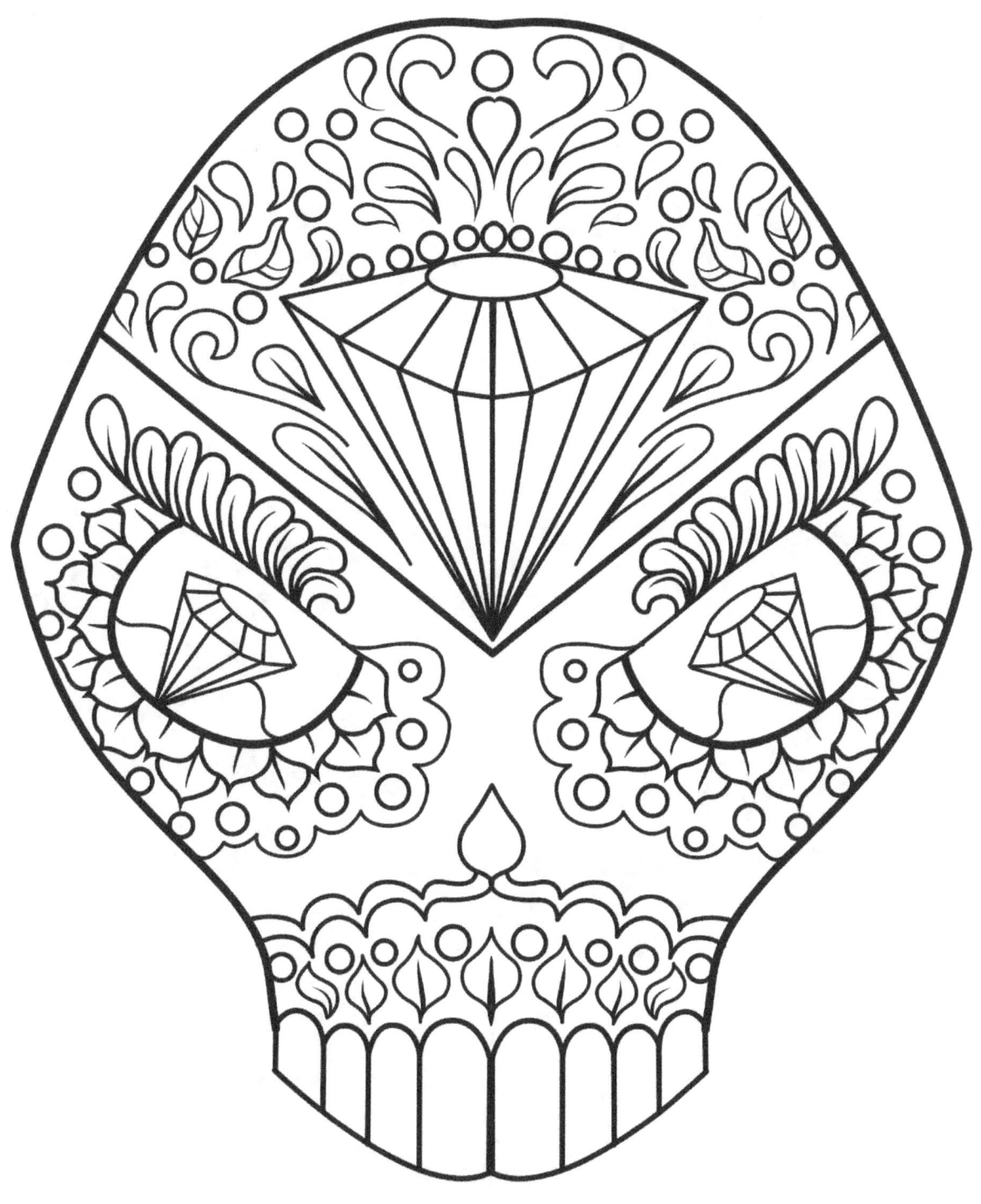

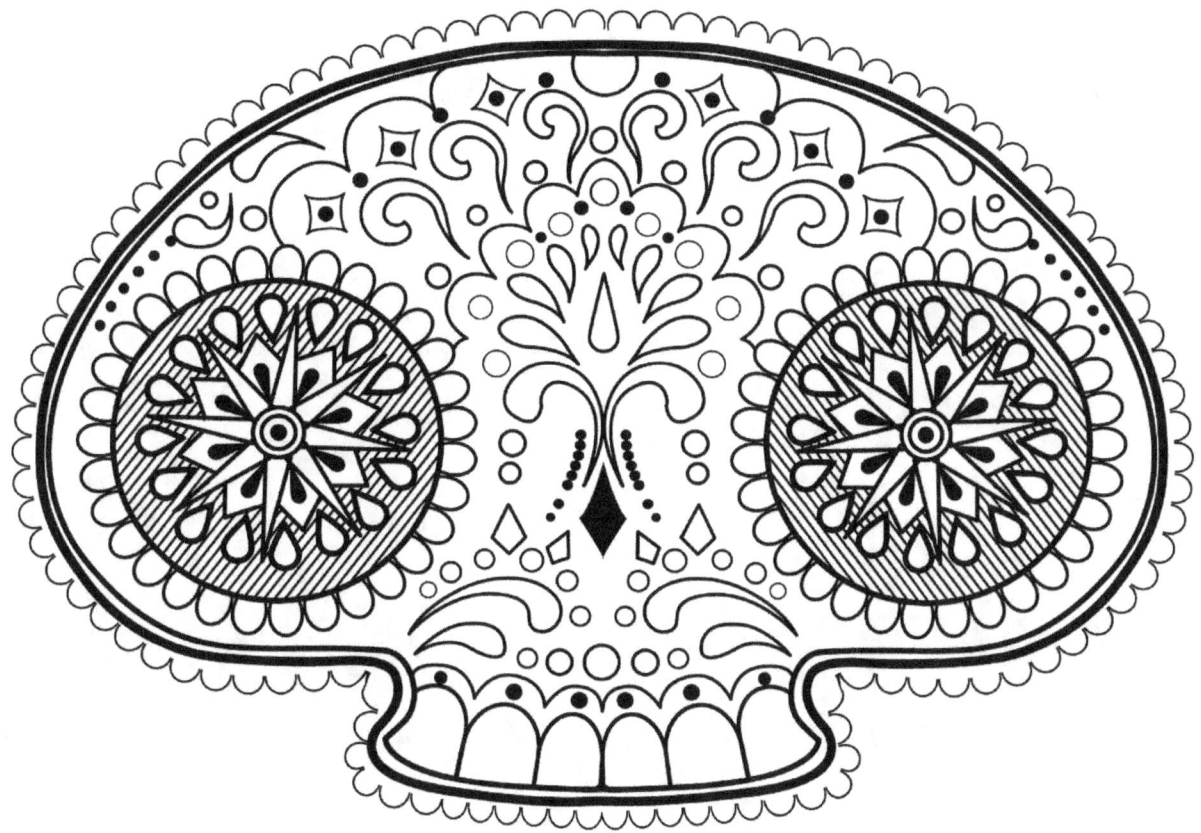

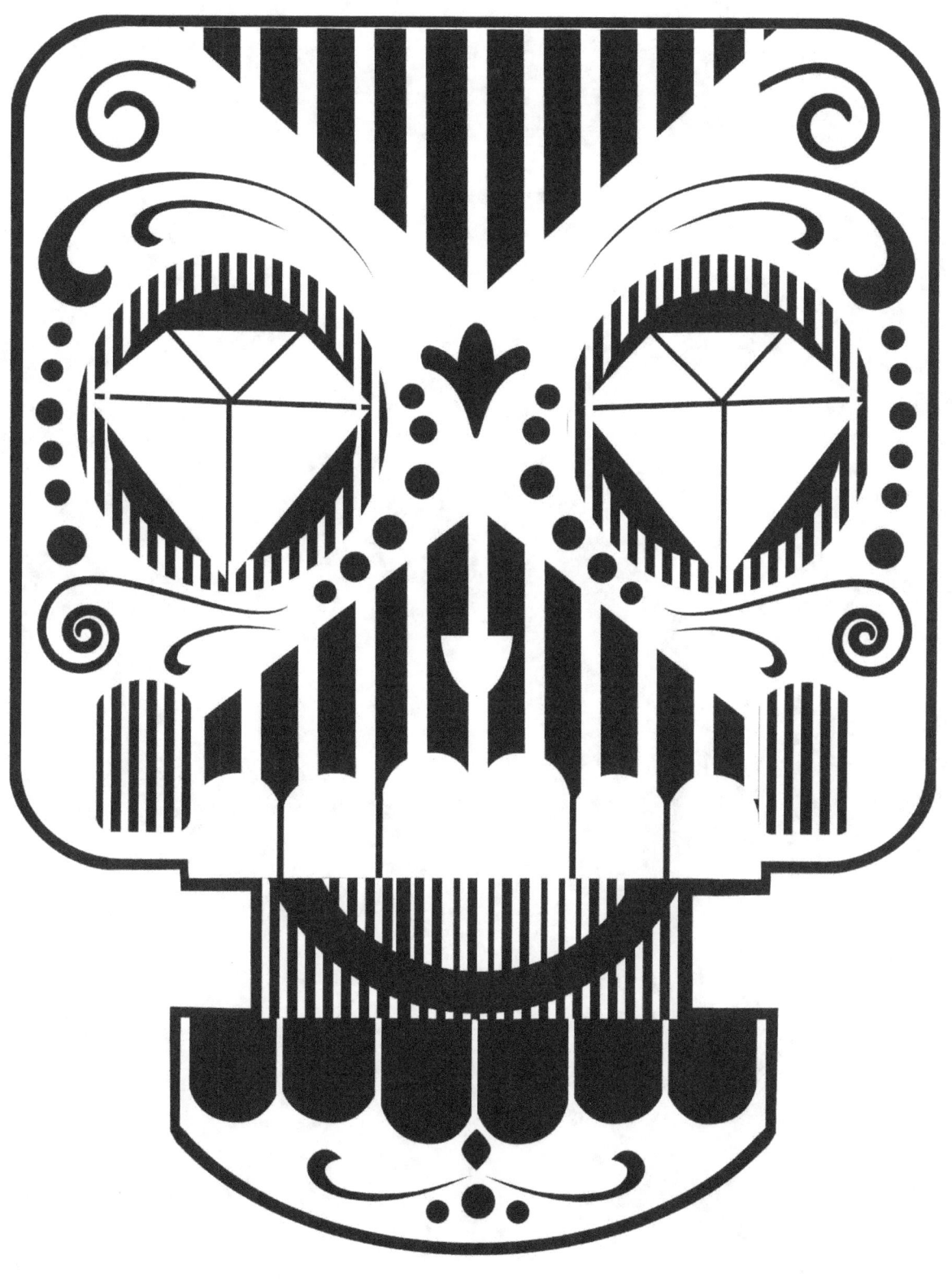

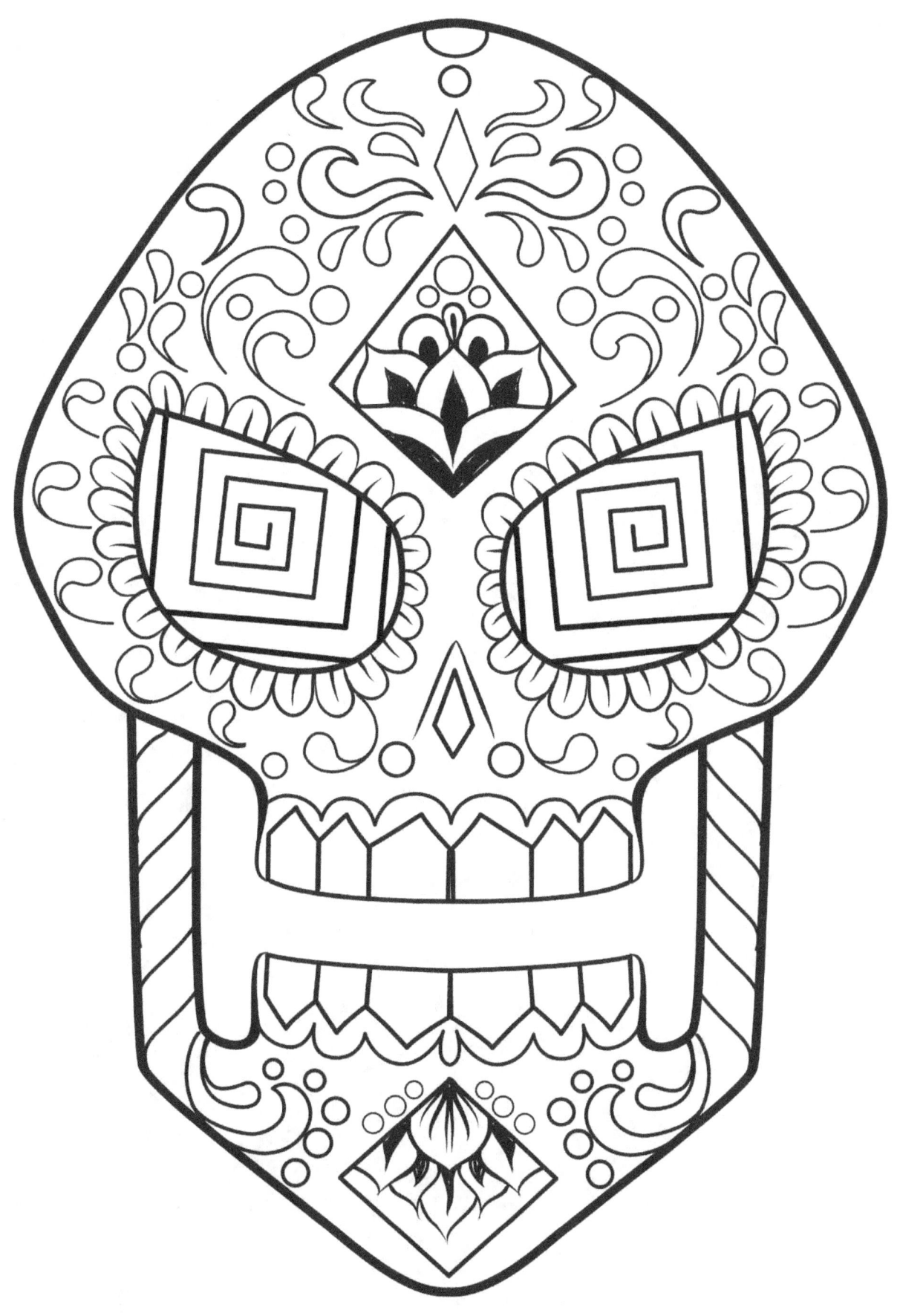

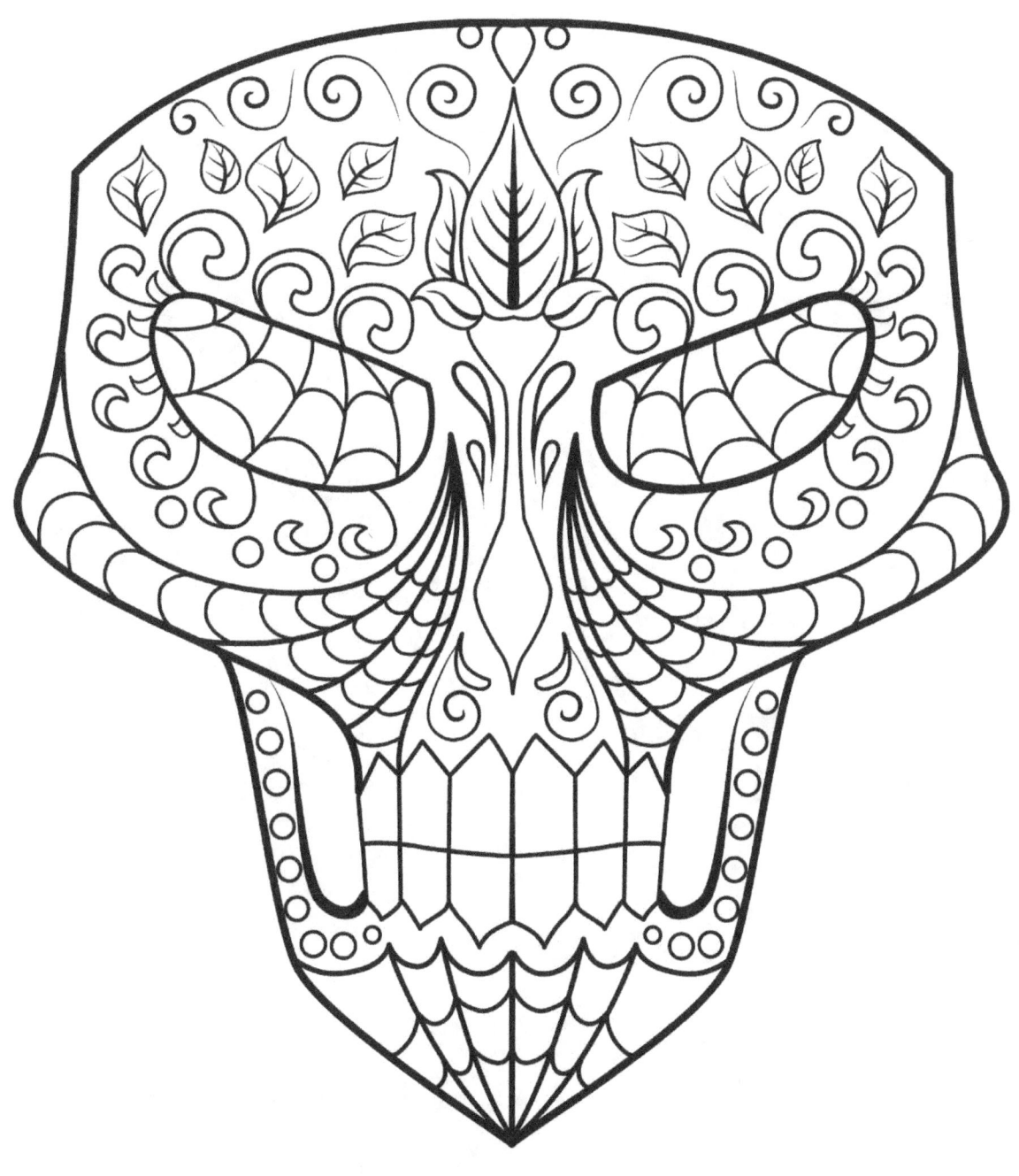

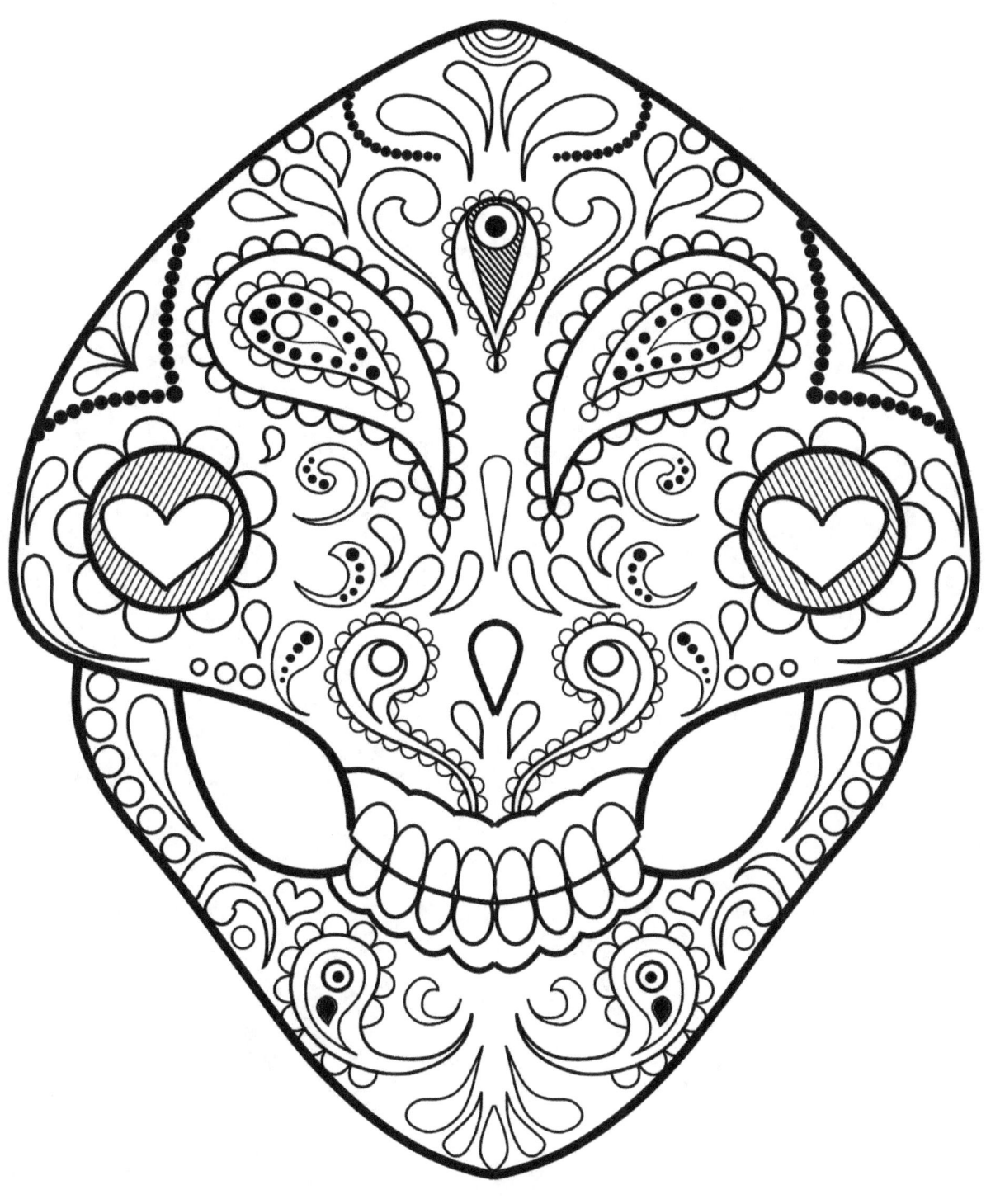

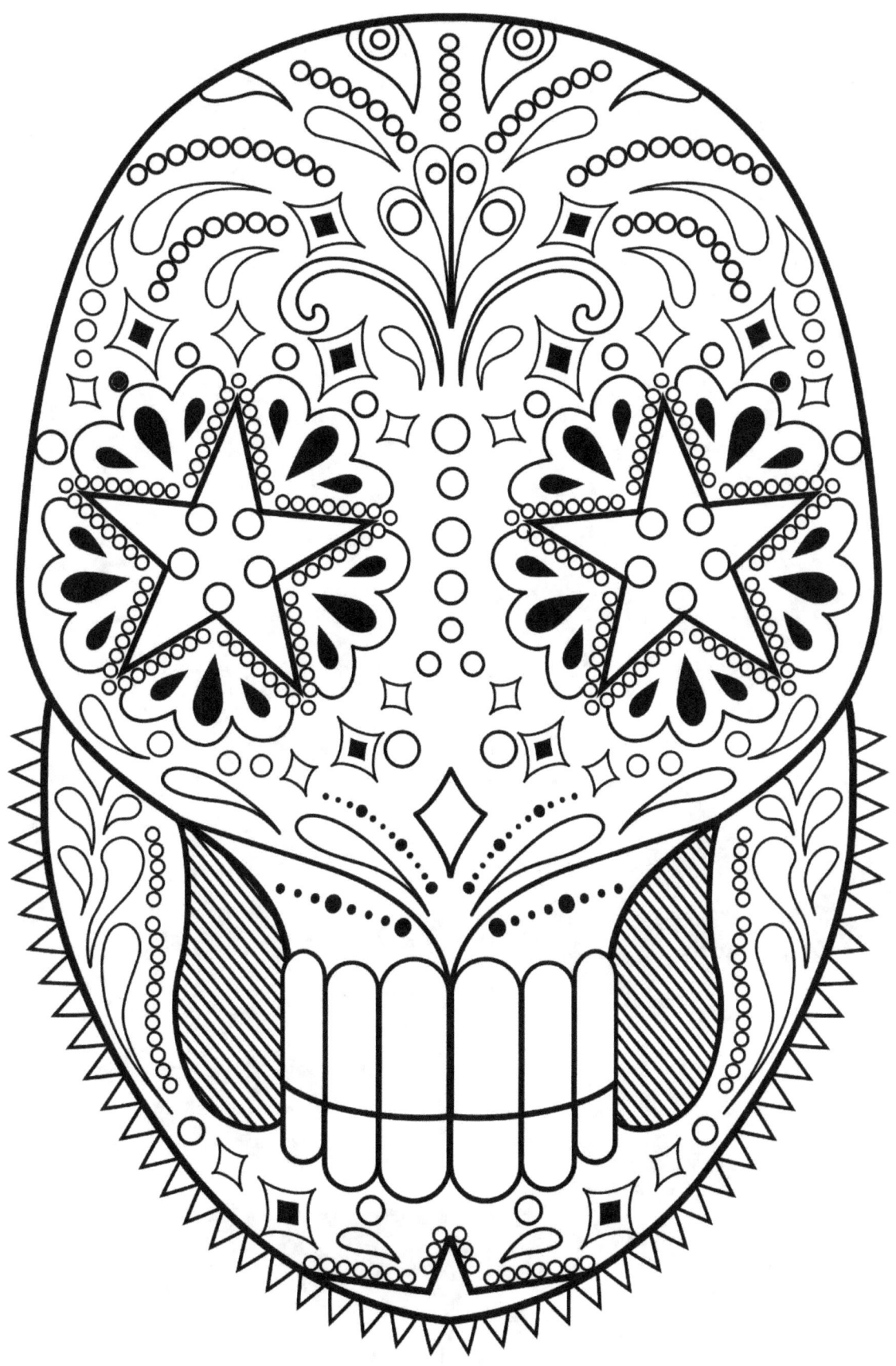

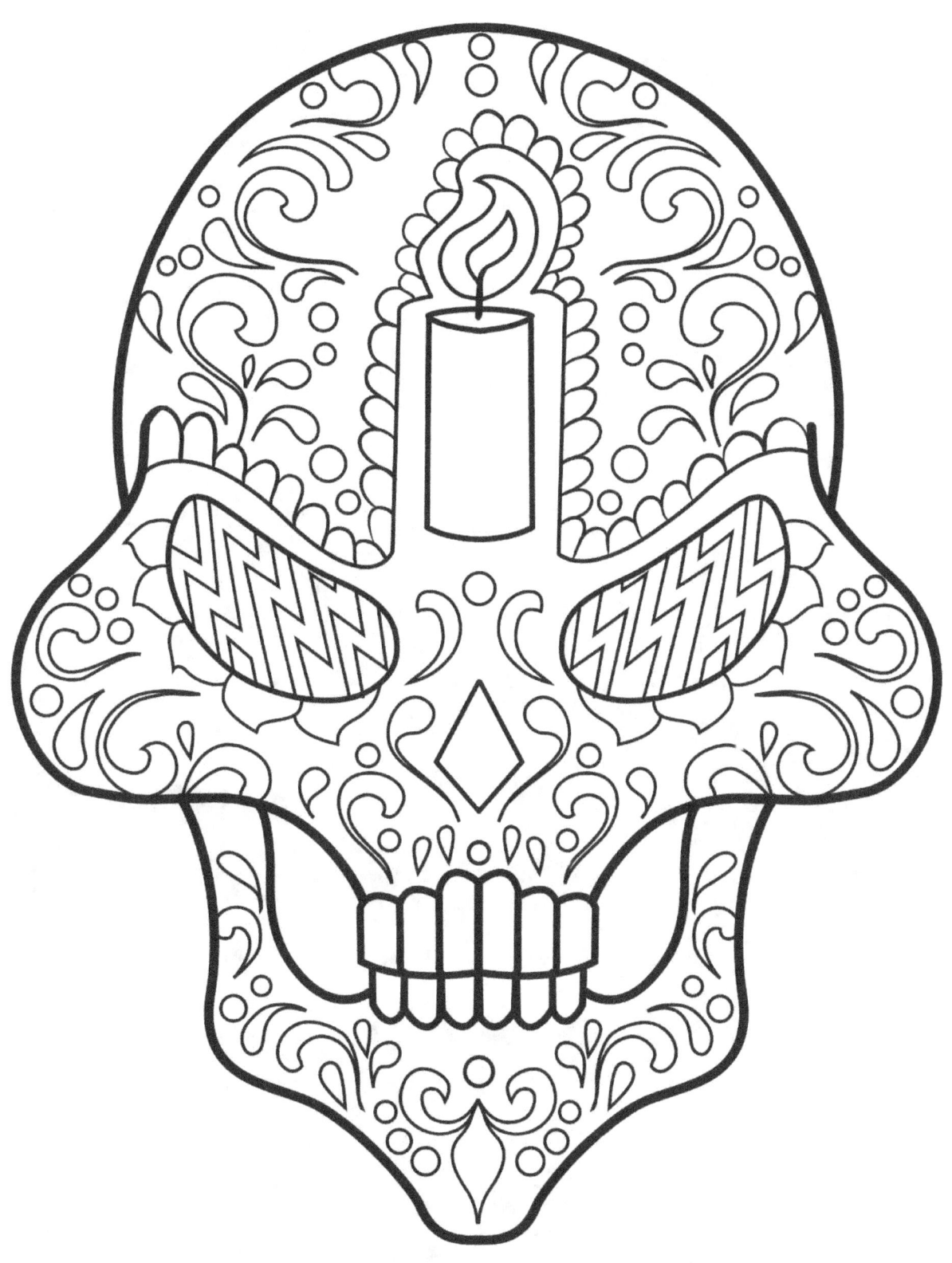

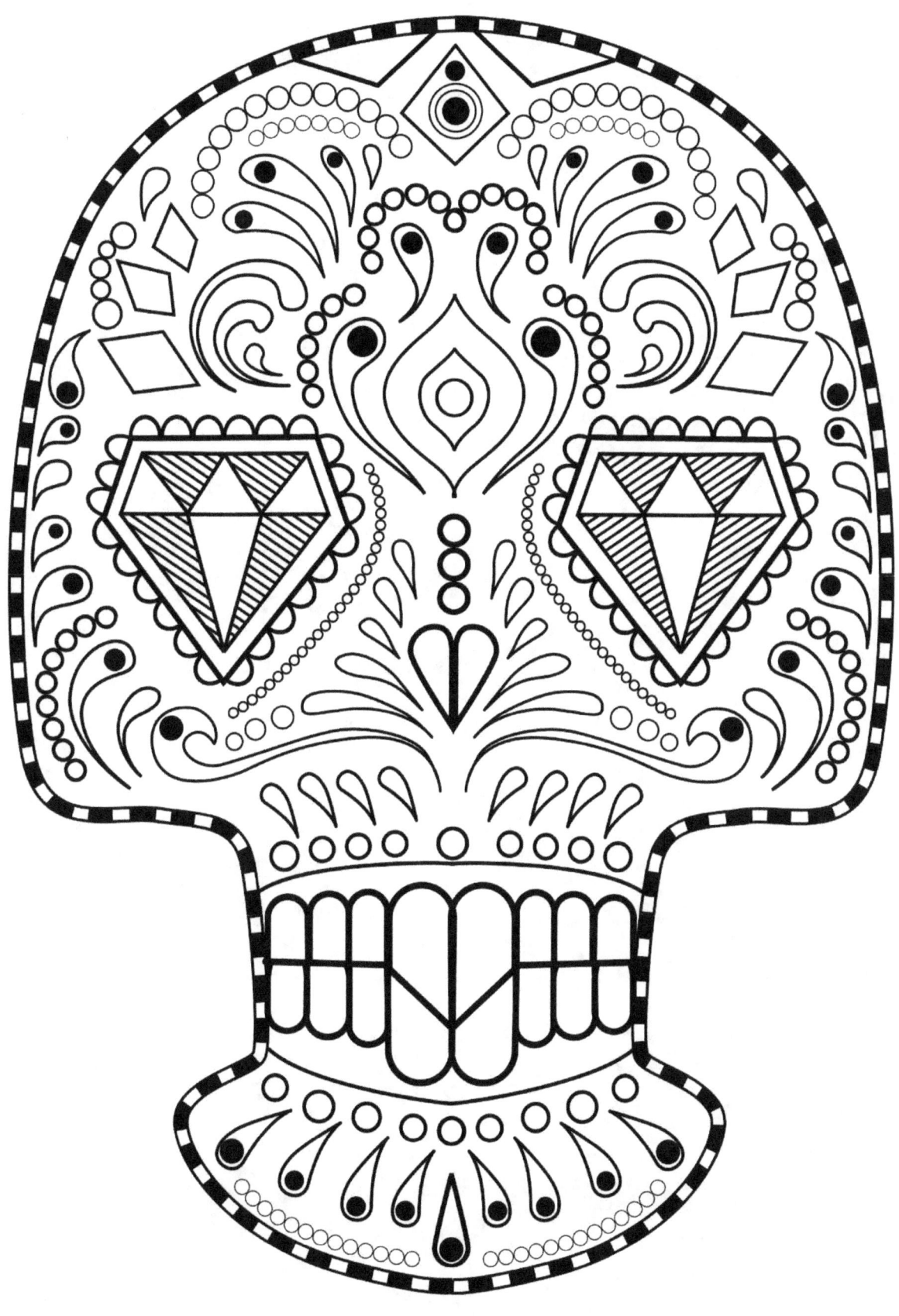

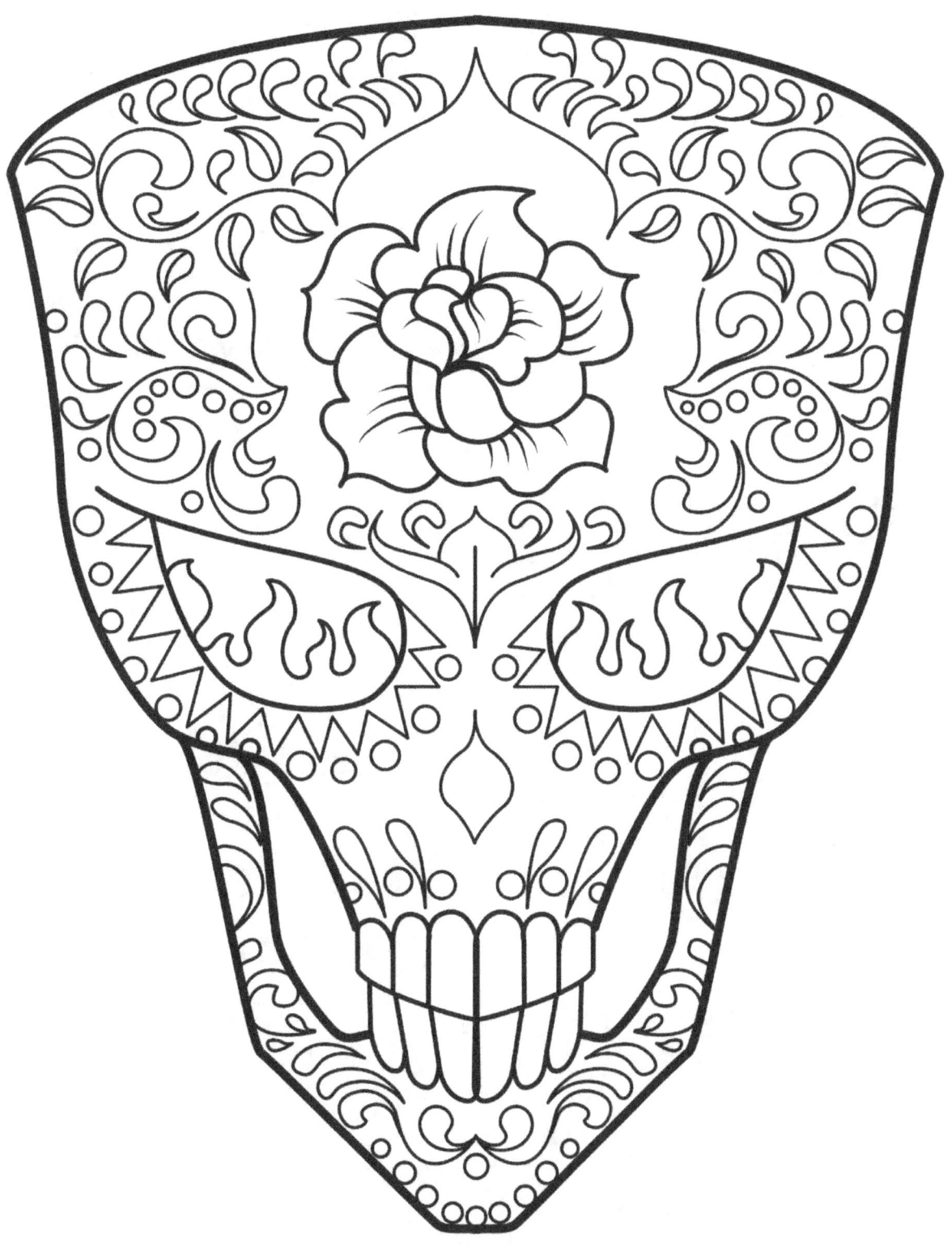

# ABOUT THE AUTHOR

Shannon Duffy lives in Southern California with her two sons and the occasional stray animal that may show up from time to time. While still in high school, she enrolled in a Chicano Studies course at a local college and from that began her interest in all things sugar skull related. She has amassed quite the collection of sugar skull themed art from around the globe and enjoys making sugar skulls with her family.

Some of her other book credits include If You Wore the Uniform... You're a Brown (Volume 1), The Couples Guide to Pregnancy & Beyond, Stormy Knight: Prom Queen of the Undead, Do Butterflies Have Noses?, Lazy Larry, Let's Learn About the Bat, Let's Learn About the Seahorse, Let's Learn About the Dragonfly, Let's Learn About the Ladybug, The Way Cool Intergalactic Space Book and Sugar Skulls Design and Coloring Book.

Her official author website is: www.ShannonMarieDuffy.com

If you enjoyed this book, be sure to pick up a copy of Sugar Skulls Design and Coloring Book. It's the first in the series and it features more traditional sugar skull designs. It's available wherever books are sold.

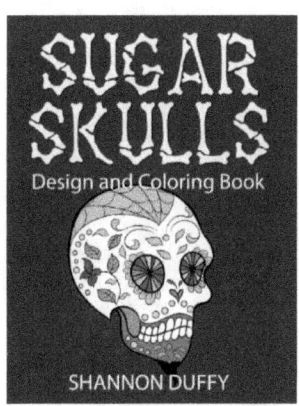

www.ingramcontent.com/pod-product-compliance
Lightning Source LLC
Chambersburg PA
CBHW081839170526
45167CB00007B/2847